PARTICIPATIVE MANAGEMENT
QUALITY OF WORKLIFE
AND JOB ENRICHMENT

Participative Management
Quality of Worklife
and Job Enrichment

Edited by Richard B. Miller

NOYES DATA CORPORATION

Park Ridge, New Jersey, U.S.A.

1977

Foreword

This is the first volume in our *Management Review Series*. These reviews will furnish definitive texts and treatments of relevant subjects, where most of the available literature is either inadequate or difficult to acquire. It is hoped that the books will meet the needs of organizations which are finding it costly and time consuming to generate information from scratch.

Richard B. Miller, who is responsible for this first volume, is managing editor of *The Bankers Magazine* and a master of his chosen assignment which has held his interest for many years.

This is a book about new and basically different management systems, which have been tested and found profitable for both company and workers. It describes conditions in which worker participation in management provides enrichment in the quality of worklife for employees and increased productivity benefitting management. It discusses the various kinds of rewards and satisfactions which people seek in their jobs. Many of these gratifications can be provided by a forward-looking management dedicated to the proposition that job enrichment, carefully planned, will prove mutually beneficial to workers, management, shareholders and consumers alike.

Each chapter is based on real-life situations and can be read with profit by those whose interest has been aroused in the subject, particularly by those whose interest has led them to the point where they are anxious to discover whether their own company can improve the quality of its employees' worklife by some sort of participative management and/or enrichment technique. The book will also serve as a handbook for those who, already committed to such a plan, need detailed knowledge of the mechanics of the system and the problems likely to arise. Needless to say, such problems are anticipated and discussed in detail.

Contents

Introduction

The material in this chapter is based on "Improving the Quality of Worklife . . . and in the Process, Improving Productivity," prepared for the Manpower Administration, U.S. Department of Labor, by Edward M. Glaser, Human Interaction Institute, and published as PB 236 209, August 1974.

The quality of worklife consists of many things. Harvard Professor Richard E. Walton[1] proposes the following eight major conceptual categories to provide a framework for analyzing its salient features:

1. Adequate and fair compensation.
2. Safe and healthy working conditions.
3. Immediate opportunity to use and develop human capacities.
4. Future opportunity for continued growth and security.
5. Social integration in work organization.
6. Constitutionalism or the "rule of law" in the work organization.
7. Work and the total life space (this refers to concern that the employing organization avoid *imposing* demands that seriously affect the employee's ability to perform other life roles, such as spouse or parent).
8. The social relevance of worklife.

Some of these conceptual categories tend to be positively correlated and some other pairs, such as numbers 5 and 6, tend to oppose each other. And different types of work groups may have different priorities of values.

If management did nothing more, however, than sincerely invite the people who work at a particular task to suggest ways to improve their operation and the quality of their worklife; if these ideas were received in a spirit of appreciation; if the employees were then asked to participate in studying the feasibility and recommending appropriate means of implementing each suggestion that survives such review—the quality of life at work probably would be enhanced. Further, there is evidence that productivity often would increase in the process. Still further, a style of management practice that manifests concern about job enrichment, employee security, career opportunities, and opportunities for employees to have voice in matters which affect them is entirely consistent with meticulously controlled operations in the interest of efficiency, effectiveness, quality assurance, customer service, profitability—*and* high employee morale.

It is not to be confused with some abstract sociopolitical concept of "democratic management." Managers who evidence such concern continue to be accountable for carrying out their responsibilities effectively. If they learn that inviting consultation or "collective wisdom" in appropriate kinds of problem solving or decision making from the persons they supervise is likely to lead to better quality and acceptance of those solutions or decisions, then they simply become better managers.

A CASE IN POINT

In early 1973, three months after management gave employees at the Kaiser Steel mill in Fontana, California, responsibility for saving the plant, which was threatened with shutdown because of inability to compete with Japanese imports and thus was losing money, there was an astonishing 32.1 percent increase in productivity.

The *Los Angeles Times* quoted one worker's observations on reasons for this jump.

> Look, before, nobody paid any attention to a guy and so he figured why in hell should he pay attention to the pipe . . . . People finally paid attention to the men, the boss started listening, the man on the next machine started looking around, and pretty soon everybody got into the swing of things.

CHANGING ORIENTATIONS TOWARD WORKLIFE

In the United States and other technologically developed countries, mankind seems in the process of changing objectives and values. During the nineteenth century, the goal of economic emancipation gradually was superseded by that of political liberty. Next came the quest for a higher standard of living, coupled in recent years with a growing concern for social justice. Added to this list of goals is another concern, one which has manifested itself recently with greater sharpness: a demand to enhance the quality of life at work.

Studs Terkel, in "Work Without Meaning,"[2] describes the plight of the jobholder in these terms:

> To write about work is, by the very nature of the subject, to write about violence—to the spirit as well as to the body. It is about ulcers as well as accidents, about shouting matches as well as fistfights, about nervous breakdowns as well as kicking the dog around. It is, above all (or beneath all), about daily humiliations. To survive the day is triumph enough for the walking wounded among the great many of us.
>
> The scars, psychic as well as physical, brought home to the supper table and the TV set, may have touched, malignantly, the soul of our society. More or less. ("More or less," that most ambiguous of phrases, pervades many of the conversations of working people, reflecting, perhaps, an ambiguity of attitude toward The Job. Something more than Orwellian acceptance, something less than Luddite sabotage. Often the two impulses are fused in the same person.)
>
> It is about a search, too, for daily meaning as well as daily bread, for recognition as well as cash, for astonishment rather than torpor; in short, for a sort of life rather than a Monday through Friday sort of dying. Perhaps immortality, too, is part of the quest.
>
> There are, of course, the happy few who find a savor in their daily job: the Indiana stonemason, who looks upon his work and sees that it is good; the Chicago piano

tuner, who seeks and finds the sound that delights; the bookbinder, who saves a piece of history; the Brooklyn fireman, who saves a piece of life. But don't these satisfactions, like Jude's hunger for knowledge, tell us more about the person than about his task? Perhaps. Nonetheless, there is a common attribute here: *a meaning to their work well over and beyond the reward of the paycheck.*

For the many, there is a hardly concealed discontent. The blue-collar blues is no more bitterly sung than the white-collar moan. 'I'm a machine,' says the spot-welder. 'I'm caged,' says the bank teller, and echoes the hotel clerk. 'I'm a mule,' says the steelworker. 'A monkey can do what I do,' says the receptionist. 'I'm less than a farm implement,' says the migrant worker. 'I'm an object,' says the high-fashion model. Blue collar and white call upon the identical phrase: 'I'm a robot.' 'There is nothing to talk about,' the young accountant despairingly enunciates. . . .

As the automated pace of our jobs wipes out name and face—and, in many instances, feeling—there is a sacrilegious question being asked these days. To earn one's bread by the sweat of one's brow has always been the lot of mankind. At least, ever since Eden's slothful couple was served with an eviction notice. The scriptural precept was never doubted, not out loud. No matter how demanding the task, no matter how it dulls the senses and breaks the spirit, one must work. Or else.

Lately there has been a *questioning of this 'work ethic', especially by the young.* Strangely enough, it has touched off profound grievances in others, hitherto devout, silent, and anonymous. Unexpected precincts are being heard from in a show of discontent. Communiqués from the assembly line are frequent and alarming: absenteeism. On the evening bus, the tense, pinched faces of young file clerks and elderly secretaries tell us more than we care to know. On the expressways, middle management men pose without grace behind their wheels as they flee city and job.

There are other means of showing it, too. Inchoately,

sullenly, it appears in slovenly work, in the put-down of craftsmanship. A farm equipment worker in Moline complains that the careless worker who turns out more that is bad is better regarded than the careful craftsman who turns out less that is good. The first is an ally of the Gross National Product. The other is a threat to it, a kook—and the sooner he is penalized the better. Why, in these circumstances, should a man work with care? Pride does indeed precede the face. . . .

The drones are no longer invisible nor mute. Nor are they exclusively of one class. Markham's Man with Hoe may be Ma Bell's girl with the headset. . . . They're in the office as well as the warehouse; at the manager's desk as well as the assembly line; at some 'estranged' company's computer as well as some 'estranged' woman's kitchen floor.

Concern with life on the job is not new. The increased ferment of union activities in the 1930s and 1940s, through collective bargaining and legislation, led to improved conditions. Even before that, labor was vigorously protesting management attempts to change the work environment. In a 1915 study requested by Congress, Chicago University professor Robert F. Hoxie reported how the unions, particularly the machinists, were fighting scientific management techniques. So-called scientific management, labor complained, condemned the workers to a monotonous routine, destroyed their creativity and drove them to the brink of nervous exhaustion.

Today's aspirations for an improved worklife, however, go well beyond continuing efforts to improve benefits and working conditions. Workers are now questioning traditional managerial prerogatives. They seek, as UAW Vice President Irving Bluestone put it, "more meaningful ways and means to participate in the decision-making process that directly or indirectly affects their welfare."

This new questioning is not limited to workers. Cornell Professor Jaroslav Vanek wrote: "The quest of men to participate in the determination and decision of activities in which they are actively involved is one of the most important sociopolitical phenomena of our times."

College students have won a greater degree of self-determination in the administration of the education system—sometimes even taking part in policy formulation. Minority groups have fought for equal opportunities. Youth has gained a greater degree of freedom from parents and other adult authorities. Citizen groups and environmentalists have called for more corporate responsibility, at the expense of profits if necessary. Many companies are responding with thoughtful plans and tangible actions.

Over a large part of the world, the style of behavioral response to personal or group feelings of frustration has changed discernibly from a fatalistic acceptance of one's lot in life to a thrust for change through confrontation politics.

Ever since Adam bit into the apple people have experienced discontent and dissatisfaction. Now, an increasing percentage want to express this, often militantly.

At the same time, the dominant powers-that-be seem reluctant to risk direct confrontation. Negotiate, bargain and—if necessary—accommodate tends to be the order of the day.

Another force to be reckoned with is a rising level of expectations for a higher standard of living, especially among American workers and consumers, coupled with a rising educational level of the work force. In earlier times a worker felt lucky just to have a job, since others were waiting at the gate ready and eager to take his place. Nowadays people demand more.

At one major auto company, for example, 4,000 newly hired men did not stay through the first day on the job. And this was in a year (1969) when local unemployment rates were between 8 and 9%. This would not have happened in the thirties, no matter what was wrong with working conditions. As Eli Ginzberg[3] has observed, ". . . the combination of more education, less fear of unemployment, and higher family income is loosening the monolithic relationship that existed for so long between people and work. In an earlier day men had to work in order to eat. That is less true today."

NOTES

1. *Sloan Management Review*, Fall 1973.
2. Business and Society Review/Innovation, Spring 1974. The article is based on Mr. Terkels' book, *Working: People Talk About What They Do All Day and How They Feel About What They Do.*
3. *The Worker and the Job*, p. 70.

Motivation and Productivity

The material in this chapter is based on "Improving the Quality of Worklife . . . and in the Process, Improving Productivity," prepared for the Manpower Administration, U.S. Department of Labor, by Edward M. Glaser, Human Interaction Institute, and published as PB 236 209, August 1974.

As the organization of human effort at work becomes more specialized and compartmentalized, the worker grows even more remote from the end result of production. Only a few individuals—artists, writers, craftsmen—can turn out a complete product or service without a good deal of interdependence upon the inputs of others.

Usually only an integrated pattern of component activities provides finished goods or services. And the task of integrating a complex pattern requires management. That, in turn, calls for the assumption of managerial responsibility, which traditionally has taken the form of more or less continuous supervision and control, thereby minimizing the independence of workers.

Specialization is almost unavoidable in a technological society. And it must be remembered that specialization has enabled us to obtain many things that most of us value and otherwise could not have. But, as Aristotle observed, "Vice may be defined as the excess or deficiency of that which in adequate amounts would constitute virtue." In the pursuit of mass production techniques, our society also has generated oversimplified fragmented jobs that many employees find boring and unfit for either the human spirit or the human body. However, it should be noted that some individuals do prefer routine tasks they feel they can handle with no strain and minimal pressures of responsibility.

8

Added to the trend toward restrictive, repetitive specialization is the fact that many managers see the individual employee as nothing more than a replaceable production component in the impersonal system. Obviously, such a depersonalized view of the individual does not tap his potential for ego-involved commitment on the job.

Thus we have the ingredients for deterioration of satisfaction: boredom, alienation and hostility on the part of many workers who want to do a good job and want to feel ego-involved. These are factors related to low productivity, poor workmanship, increasing absenteeism—and sometimes sabotage—on the part of a growing number of workers.

WHAT EMPLOYEES WANT

In today's world there are a growing number of alternatives to unsatisfying employment—living on welfare or unemployment benefits, parental largesse, or that street tactic called hustling. Still, American youth has not altogether rejected the work ethic. In a 1971 survey of *college* students conducted by Daniel Yankelovich,[1] 61% expressed interest in a practical career orientation, and 75% believed collecting welfare is immoral for a person who can work. Only 30% said they would welcome less emphasis in the United States on hard work.

The work ethic does appear to be changing, however. Among *noncollege* youth—the majority—Yankelovich interprets his study data as indicating that:

> Today's young people are less fearful of economic insecurity than in the past. They want interesting and challenging work, but they assume that their employers cannot—or will not—provide it. By their own say-so, they are inclined to take 'less crap' than older workers. They are not as automatically loyal to the organization as their fathers, and they are far more cognizant of their own needs and rights. Nor are they as awed by organizational and hierarchical authority. Being less fearful of 'discipline' and the threat of losing their jobs, they feel

free to express their discontent in myriad ways, from fooling around on the job to sabotage. They are better educated than their parents, even without a college degree. They want more freedom and will bargain hard to keep their options open. A bitter fight over the right to refuse mandatory overtime, for example, does not mean that young workers will not work overtime. It does mean that the freedom to say 'no' assumes symbolic significance as an expression of freedom and autonomy. Moreover, if the work itself is not meaningful to them, they will opt for 'thirty and out' forms of retirement, shorter work weeks, frequent absenteeism, more leisure, and other methods for cutting back and cutting down on their job commitment.

Further evidence that people now want more satisfaction from the job and better resources to get the job done can be derived from the 1971 Working Conditions Survey.[2] The survey, carried out by the University of Michigan, asked a representative 1,533 American workers at all occupational levels to weigh job facets and report whether the item was: (a) very important, (b) somewhat important, (c) not too important, or (d) not at all important. The findings are shown in Table 2.1.

TABLE 2.1: PERCENTAGE OF WORKERS RATING JOB FACETS AS "VERY IMPORTANT" TO THEM

Job Facet	All workers (N=1500)*		White-collar workers (N=730)*		Blue-collar workers (N=685)*, **	
	%	Rank Order	%	Rank Order	%	Rank Order
Resources						
I receive enough help and equipment to get the job done	68	2	64	4	72	1
I have enough information to get the job done	68	2	67	3	68	2
My responsibilities are clearly defined	61	7	58	7	65	4
My supervisor is competent in doing his job	61	7	60	6	63	6

(continued)

TABLE 2.1: (continued)

Job Facet	All workers (N=1500)*		White-collar workers (N=730)*		Blue-collar workers (N=685)*, **	
	%	Rank Order	%	Rank Order	%	Rank Order
Financial Rewards						
The pay is good	64	4	57	8	72	1
The job security is good	62	6	54	10	72	1
My fringe benefits are good	51	10	40	14	62	7
Challenge						
The work is interesting	73	1	78	1	68	2
I have enough author-ity to do my job	65	3	67	3	64	5
I have an opportunity to develop my special abilities	64	4	69	2	57	9
I can see the results of my work	62	6	60	6	64	5
I am given a chance to do the things I do best	54	8	54	10	55	10
I am given a lot of free-dom to decide how I do my work	53	9	56	9	50	11
The problems I am asked to solve are hard enough	30	16	31	17	29	17
Relations with Co-workers						
My co-workers are friendly and helpful	63	5	61	5	67	3
I am given a lot of chances to make friends	44	12	39	15	49	12
Comfort						
I have enough time to get the job done	54	8	48	11	60	8
The hours are good	51	10	41	13	62	7
Travel to and from work is convenient	46	11	42	12	50	11

(continued)

TABLE 2.1:   (continued)

Job Facet	All workers (N=1500)*		White-collar workers (N=730)*		Blue-collar workers (N=685)*, **	
	%	Rank Order	%	Rank Order	%	Rank Order
Physical surroundings are pleasant	40	13	32	16	48	13
I am free from con-flicting demands that other people make of me	33	14	26	19	40	14
I can forget about my personal problems	31	15	26	18	35	15
I am not asked to do excessive amounts of work	23	17	16	20	30	16

*Base N's vary slightly from row to row because of missing data.
**Farm workers have been excluded.

If work conditions are growing in importance, this does not mean that income is irrelevant! In a study of what elements of work needed improvement most, union leaders[3] ranked pay first and job content aspects lower. But many workers also are finding it important to be allowed to work more effectively, to have some control over their job environment, and to feel that they and their work are important—the twin ingredients of self-esteem.

WORKER MOTIVATION, SATISFACTION AND EFFECTIVENESS

Three decades ago, Harvard University Professor Gordon Allport nicely expressed a key psychological consideration bearing upon the quality of worklife in what is now regarded as a classic paper:[4]

> When the work situation in which the individual finds himself realistically engages the status-seeking mo-tive—when the individual is busily engaged in using his talents, understanding his work and having pleasant

social relations with foreman and fellow worker—then he is, as the saying goes, 'identified' with his job. He likes his work; he is absorbed in it; he is productive. In McGregor's term, he is industrially *active*. That is to say, he is participant.

When on the other hand, the situation is such that the status-motive has no chance of gearing itself into the external cycles of events, when the individual goes through motions that he does not find meaningful, when he does not really participate—then comes rebellion against authority, complaints, griping, gossip, rumor, scapegoating and disaffection of all sorts. The job satisfaction is low. In McGregor's term, under such circumstances the individual is not active; he is industrially *reactive*.

. . .The problem before us is whether the immense amount of reactivity shown in business offices and factories, in federal bureaus and schools, can be reduced. . . We are learning some of the conditions in which reactivity does decline. . . . Patronizing handouts and wage-incentive systems alone do not succeed. Opportunities for consultation on personal problems are . . . found to be important; and group decision, open discussion and the retraining of leaders in accordance with democratic standards yield remarkable results. . . . In other words, a person ceases to be reactive and contrary in respect to a desirable course of conduct only when he himself has had a hand in declaring that course of conduct to be desirable. Such findings add up to the simple proposition that people must have a hand in saving themselves; they cannot and will not be saved from the outside.

The question is how to translate Allport's insights into practicality. How, in other words, do we best utilize human resources to optimize each person's potential?

Complex issues such as what may be involved in attitudes toward work and life cannot, of course, be fathomed by simplistic survey poll questions which do not probe the full flavor of reasons behind a response.

In some cases there have been dramatic breakdowns of organizational functioning such as the celebrated 1972 GM Lordstown, Ohio case that shut down the Vega production line, or the less well-known strike at Chevrolet's Norwood plant that year, where auto workers walked out, not for higher wages, but (according to the union chairman at Lordstown) from frustration at not having a chance to participate in work decisions (particularly concerning the management of the speed of their assembly line). Another less well-known reason for these two walkouts was the reorganization by the corporation of its assembly operations into the General Motors Assembly Department, which called for the union to merge seniority lists of separate locals that hitherto had been autonomous. This clash in "property rights" over seniority frequently has led to acute conflicts that more often than not result in a strike.

In April 1973, Gallup released a poll bearing upon productivity. Gallup interviewed a representative sample of U.S. wage earners and found:

> Half of all wage earners say they could accomplish more each day if they tried, with three in five of this group indicating they could increase their output by 20% or more.
>
> The percentage who say they could get more work done is highest (61%) among young adults in the work force—those between the ages of 18 and 29. Men are more likely to state they could accomplish more than are female earners.

Here are the questions asked of wage earners and the results:

> Some persons claim that American Workers are not turning out as much work each day as they should. Do you agree or disagree with this?
>
> Workers Could Produce More
>
> Agree 56%
> Disagree 33
> No Opinion 11
>
> In your own case, could you accomplish more each day if you tried?
>
> Yes 50%

No 47
No Opinion 3

How much more could you accomplish each day if you tried?

Ten percent	15%
Twenty percent	15
Thirty percent	7
Forty percent	2
Fifty percent	5
Over fifty percent	3
Don't know/No answer	3
	50%

Gallup comments: A key factor affecting productivity is job satisfaction. The worker who hates his job or is bored with it is not likely to be as productive as he could be.

A cross-tabulation of survey findings is most revealing on this point. Among those in the survey who say they are 'very satisfied' with their jobs, less than one quarter say they could do 30% or more additional work per day. In sharp contrast, among those in the survey who say they are 'very dissatisfied' with their jobs, about four in ten (two-fifths) say they could do 30% or more additional work per day.

Aside from job satisfaction studies and considerations, there is a preponderance of evidence suggesting legitimate concern with factors that might alienate or motivate people at work. These factors do have a direct bearing on costs, productivity, craftsmanship and loss of jobs in the U.S. to foreign competitors who can produce for less—often with better quality.

It seems fruitless to argue over the degree of discontent among workers. Variables such as the age of the worker, the expectations he (or she) brings to the job, and the difference between the economic and psychological satisfactions people seek from their work are among the factors that bear upon degree of job satisfaction. *The important point on which many people—managers, as well as workers and union leaders—can agree is that a pragmatic effort to improve the American workplace for the benefit of all constituents or all concerned (customers, the company, task groups, individual workers, labor unions and stockholders) is a valid, worthwhile objective.*

PRODUCTIVITY—CONCEPT AND RAMIFICATIONS

To many an employee, the word productivity connotes some sort of exploitative pressure from above to speed up output per man-hour. It suggests efficiency experts, work force reductions and even layoffs. This has been true in several cases where efforts to improve productivity have focused on cost reduction. Perhaps because of this, some labor union leaders see productivity improvement efforts and broader attempts to enhance the quality of work as a trick on the part of management to circumvent collective bargaining and thereby weaken unions.

It is interesting to note in this context that union cooperation with management to improve productivity can be found. Bruce Thrasher, an assistant to the president of the United States Steelworkers of America, strongly disagreed with the social scientists, pollsters and journalists who talked of a growing alienation from work by the American labor force. Like a number of other union leaders, Thrasher considered attempts to counter this alienation by job enrichment outside collective bargaining as an effort to attenuate the role of labor unions.

Yet, during a conference on the work ethic, when Thrasher was asked what objection he as a union leader had to the reportedly splendid 32% improvement in productivity results achieved at the Kaiser-Fontana pipe plant, he replied, "None. I have been part of the Steelworkers Committee that developed the Fontana plan. That was accomplished in collaboration with the union, with no violation of contract provisions and no speedup. Now, if you want to focus on how to improve productivity without manipulating or trying to take advantage of labor, and experiment in sincere partnership with the union, we're for that."

It should be recognized that labor productivity is only one among many factors involved in overall productivity. But in many cases it is a crucial one. People who can easily grasp the ideas of improved technology often find it less easy to understand the mechanics and psychological dynamics of labor productivity.

The real meaning of productivity is to produce more (or rather optimally, if the baseline level was sub-optimal) with the same amount of human effort. To oversimplify a little, labor productivity measurement is the efficiency with which output is produced by the resources utilized. It refers to either man-hours worked or total hours paid for measurable labor output.

This concept is illustrated by a clause in the 1950 management-labor agreement between General Motors and the UAW:

> The improvement factor provided herein recognizes that a continuing improvement in the standard of living of employees depends upon technological progress, better tools, methods, processes, equipment, and a co-operative attitude on the part of all parties in such progress. It further recognizes the principle that to produce more with the same amount of human effort is a sound economic and social objective.

As former General Motors Board Chairman, Richard Gerstenberg, pointed out in his speech before the American Newspaper Publishers Association:

> Productivity is not a matter of making employees work longer or harder. Increased productivity results mostly from sound planning, from wise investment, from new technology, from better techniques, from greater efficiency—in short, from the better exercise of the functions of management. . . . Beyond this, productivity depends upon the conscientious effort of every employee, a willingness to do a fair day's work for a fair day's wage. If America is to improve its productivity—and we must—then productivity must be everybody's job.

NOTES

1. D. Yankelovich, Inc., *The Changing Values on Campus.* (New York: Washington Square Press, March 1972).
2. Survey Research Center, University of Michigan, *Survey of Working Conditions.* (Washington, D.C., U.S. Department of Labor, Employment Standards Administration, August 1971).
3. H.L.S. Shephard and N. Q. Herrick, *Where Have All the Robots Gone?* (New York: The Free Press, 1972.)
4. C. W. Allport, "The Psychology of Participation," *Psychological Review* 52 (1945) 117-132.

The Role of the Supervisor
in the Quality of Worklife

The material in this chapter is based on "Improving the Quality of Work Life Managerial Practices," prepared for the U.S. Department of Labor by George Strauss, and published as PB 255 047, June 1975.

The supervisor is one key to the quality of worklife. A University of Michigan study (Survey Research Center, 1971) which sought to relate a large number of characteristics of workers' jobs to overall satisfaction illustrates the wide variety of ways by which supervisory behavior impacts on subordinate satisfaction. The eight most closely related factors are listed below:

1. Having a "nurturant" supervisor
2. Receiving adequate help, assistance, etc.
3. Having few "labor standards problems" (such as safety hazards, poor hours, or poor transportation)
4. Fair promotional policies
5. Supervisor not supervising too closely
6. Having a technically competent supervisor
7. Autonomy in matters affecting work
8. A job with "enriching" demands

Of the eight, three refer directly to the supervisor (nos. 1, 5, and 6), three are often primarily his responsibility (nos. 2, 7, and 8), and even the last two (nos. 3 and 4) are substantially subject to his influence.

As we have seen, the supervisor influences quality of work life directly and indirectly. He affects subordinates *directly* through his daily interaction with them. He can be supportive ("nurturant") or not understanding, friendly or distant, available to provide help or always busy, he can supervise closely or permit autonomy, he can make technically competent or incompetent decisions—and so forth. Whatever he does has its inevitable impact on satisfaction and productivity (though, as we shall see, the relative importance of the supervisor's attitudes and behavior may vary considerably from situation to situation).

Equally important, in most instances, is the supervisor's indirect impact as a participant in the design and management of various environmental and work systems, including those discussed in previous chapters. He influences the design of jobs. He plays a key role in the administration of career and reward systems. And he also is in a position to foster the development of social systems. In none of these areas can the supervisor act alone; he is subject to a variety of constraints placed by higher management. Nevertheless, the alert supervisor can take a systems view which will help integrate these factors—and a number of others—in such a fashion that quality of worklife will be enhanced as well as organizational objectives of efficiency and adaptability.

Research in this area may stress either the supervisor's day-to-day interactions or his longer-term role as a systems designer and manager. Regardless of which view one takes, the manager is concerned with maintaining both a satisfactory work environment and high levels of employee motivation.

KEY SUPERVISORY ROLES

One thing is certain: the supervisor performs functions which are critical to high quality of worklife. The two major functions are:

Consideration: This relates to the supervisor's activities in providing a satisfactory work environment—to the way he treats his employees on a day-to-day basis, his personal relations with them, his approach to the disciplinary process and the like. In terms of the University of Michigan survey just mentioned the considerate supervisor is "nurturant," and this factor heads the list as being closely linked to overall job satisfaction.

A considerate supervisor makes even a boring job more tolerable, and consideration may be particularly important for the instrumentally oriented worker who does not seek satisfaction from the work itself. Consideration is a necessary, though not sufficient, condition for participation. Without consideration, for example, job redesign experiments are almost sure to fail. In most situations consideration affects satisfaction more than it does productivity; however, it can also influence productivity in some rather interesting ways, as will be described later on. In any case it is clearly a significant determinant of quality of worklife.

Facilitation: Items number 2 and 6 in the Michigan survey relate respectively to "receiving adequate help, assistance, etc." and "having a technically competent supervisor." Clearly, in the absence of these factors, the job will be frustrating and dissatisfying and productivity will almost certainly be low. Both factors are included in the term "facilitation." Facilitation generally includes those things which the supervisor can do to make it easier for the worker to do his job. Without facilitation, work effort is wasted—and in terms of expectancy theory there will be little likelihood that work effort will be converted into performance or lead to rewards. If consideration can be viewed as sociological support, facilitation provides technical support, although (as will be seen) the concept involves more than purely technical support, since important elements of direction, guidance, and training are included.

CONSIDERATION

One of the presumed lessons of the early Human Relations movement was that the supervisor should be considerate, that he should treat his subordinates as human beings, that he should look out for their welfare, be fair, and show interest in them as individuals, etc. Today we are less convinced than we were 25 years ago that this is all that is required to make a successful supervisor, but clearly consideration is an important element in determining quality of worklife. Regardless of what else it might do, consideration reduces the sense of oppression which the worker feels when he is confronted by the pressures, rigidities, and sterilities of his job. By providing "fair treatment" consideration helps meet management's end of the "implicit bargain" and in return for this workers are more likely to do their "fair day's work." And, further, as we shall see later, a valuable by-product of consideration is that it tends to strengthen the effort-satisfaction expectancy relationship.

"Treating people as human beings," "being fair," "showing interest in them as individuals"—all these sound like motherhood virtues (and indeed the term consideration smacks of the nurses' Tender Loving Care). It isn't that simple, however. Being a nice guy isn't enough, for the supervisor must adjust to the special needs and expectations of his group as well as those of each individual in it. A statement by an employee that his boss is "fair" may tell us as much about the employee's expectations as about the boss's actual behavior. Whether supervisory behavior in a given situation is viewed as considerate and whether it actually contributes to productivity and satisfaction depends on three factors: the subordinate's(s') expectations, the boss's actual behavior, and the subordinate's(s') perception of his behavior. Or, to put this in sociological terms: consideration is related to legitimacy—the considerate leader is one who behaves in a fashion which his subordinates feel appropriate for a supervisor.

With this introduction, let me sketch a few of the elements of consideration: creating a feeling of approval, developing personal relations, providing fair treatment and equitable rule enforcement.

Creating a Feeling of Approval

The personal, man-to-man relationships between a supervisor and his subordinates have a lot to do with the way subordinates view their jobs. Since employees are dependent on their boss, it is important for them to feel that he approves of both their work and themselves as individuals and that he is concerned with their personal development.

The supervisor can create a feeling of his approval of subordinates in many ways: taking an active interest in their home life, listening to their problems, giving praise when justified, showing tolerance when mistakes are made, and so forth. However, the psychological perception, the feeling of approval, is what is significant. The overall supervisory pattern may be more important than any one specific act. In fact, the existence of such a feeling helps determine how individual acts are interpreted.

In short, the existence of a feeling of approval permits the establishment of an exchange relationship or psychological contract. The existence of such a feeling may be interpreted as meaning that the supervisor has demonstrated a personal loyalty to his subordinates. Until he has done so, he cannot expect loyalty to flow the other way.

Note though, that approval means different things to different people.

Two lacquer-mixers who worked pretty much by themselves at opposite ends of a long factory floor were once interviewed. They did the same job and were under the same foreman (who said both did a good job). The first mixer said, "I've got a good boss. He knows I know the job, so he leaves me alone. He never bothers me." The second mixer said, "My foreman doesn't care whether I am dead or alive. He's a bum foreman who doesn't show any interest in his men or how they are doing."

What one mixer perceived as a vote of confidence, the other perceived as neglect. Support is highly idiosyncratic and is hard to capture in a few hard-and-fast rules.

Developing Personal Relations

A feeling of approval is more likely to result if the boss shows personal interest in his subordinates. After all, the organization is impersonal; only individual members of management, particularly the immediate boss, can make it personal.

The key importance of good interpersonal relations has been a major theme of human relations literature through the years. However, the earlier discussions stressed non-job-related matters. The general assumption was that good informal relations on matters that are not directly related to the job set the stage for better communications between manager and subordinate on problems related to work. After all—it was argued—an employee rarely feels completely free and easy when talking to his boss about his work, for he is quite aware that the boss is the one who hands out rewards and punishments. But when they talk about the employee's fishing trip, the employee is the expert for the time being, even if there is no true equality between them. Some of the air of permissiveness and informality created in discussing baseball or the weather carry over to on-the-job affairs. Once the manager and the subordinate know each other as individuals, both will feel freer to bring up mutual problems. Further, by acting as a careful listener the supervisor may be able to defuse family and other off-the-job problems which might be bothering the employee and disrupting the work.

So went the conventional wisdom of early human relations. However, there is another literature which warns against reducing social distance too much. In most situations a boss is expected to "be friendly" (and this is particularly true where the American tradition of equality prevails), but the meaning of friendliness varies greatly from one situation to another. Usually there are well defined expectations as to how close the relationship should be: military officers should be aloof from their men; deans should invite all new faculty to dinner but not visit their classes; plant managers are expected to make "howdy rounds" in the plant and to be good fellows at the company picnic (but perhaps only there); supervisors should show interest in their subordinate's vacation stories and in some plants (but not others) go out drinking with their men on pay day.

A wide variety of factors is relevant here. Life insurance agents feel under great pressure from their job and their boss and, as a consequence, fear that if he gets too close to them he will criticize them. At sea there is a traditional social gap between officers and men—though this is rapidly breaking down under the impact of automation. This distance is maintained by means of separate uniforms and separate eating and sleeping arrangements. Yet on smaller ships this traditional formality tends to break down. There is more of it in the navy than in the merchant marine, and on European ships (where officers and men come from different social classes) than on American ships.

Providing Fair Treatment

Since subordinates are directly dependent on their bosses, they are understandably anxious to receive fair treatment in the distribution of rewards and punishments. But what is considered fair may vary widely from one local culture to another.

In general, "being fair" involves the following elements: (a) letting the subordinate know clearly and in advance exactly what is required of him, thus reducing the frustration due to uncertainty; (b) making decisions on clearly explained grounds which can be defended as legitimate; (c) dispensing rewards in a manner which seems to make them proportional to contributions and which meets the requirements of "distributive justice"; and (d) providing some sort of appeals procedure. In terms of path-goal analysis, fairness of this sort increases the subordinate's perceptions that effort on his part will lead to his receiving valued rewards.

"Being fair" from an employee's standpoint may also mean that their bosses respect local work customs (e.g., secretaries have 20 minute coffee breaks; no one gets a rush job Christmas Eve; deans should not drop into senior faculty's classes; small items may be taken home without being considered stealing). Many of these work customs have status or symbolic meaning. Innocent decisions about parking lots or the arrangement of tables may upset delicate social relations, lead to turmoil and antagonism, and be viewed as viciously unfair.

Rules are more likely to be accepted if the workers to be affected have some chance to participate in their development. The following story illustrates this point and also suggests an approach to labor-management relations:

> The superintendent of machine operations was convinced by his Safety Department that long-sleeved shirts were a hazard even when rolled up. So he posted a notice that beginning next Monday morning wearing long sleeves on the job would be prohibited.

> Monday morning, four men showed up with long sleeves. Given the choice of working without shirts or cutting their sleeves off, they refused to do either and were sent home. The union filed a sharp grievance, asking for back pay for time lost.

Then the Personnel Department stepped in. The rule was suspended for a week and a special meeting called with the union grievance committee. The safety director explained that if a worker got his sleeve caught in a machine his whole arm might be ripped off. The union agreed to the rule provided that it was extended to management (who originally had been exempt on the grounds they didn't get close enough to the machines).

Next Monday the rule was reinstated. A few men, forgetfully, arrived in long sleeves. The other men handed them a pair of scissors and insisted that the offending sleeves be cut off on the spot. Later in the afternoon a union vice president and a company time-study man were treated in the same way. The rule was in full effect!

Equitable Rule Enforcement

The early human relations literature stressed the importance of the supervisor avoiding unfair, punitive discipline, a natural reaction to the activities of Neanderthal foreman in the dark days before the advent of unions. In unionized plants an elaborate code of "industrial jurisprudence" has evolved which provides "due process" in cases of discipline. Important elements of this code have been extended to nonunion organizations. Thus "fairness" is often viewed as requiring at the minimum that (a) punishment should be inflicted only for known rules and that the degree of punishment should not exceed expectations; (b) first offenses, unless serious, should receive only a warning, and (c) opportunities should be provided for appeals. The union grievance procedure provides an elaborate review mechanism which reduces the possibility that discipline will be applied arbitrarily or inconsistently. Many nonunion plants provide similar appeal channels.

While rules and procedures for discipline have become reasonably well codified, especially in industrial plants, there have been some experiments with new approaches to the subject which are worth mentioning here.

1. Traditional, "progressive" discipline provides for increasingly severe penalties each time an employee is disciplined, with the

sequence typically running as follows: (a) oral warning, (b) written warning, (c) layoff, and (d) discharge. Some companies have experimented with eliminating step (c) altogether, on the grounds that a stern warning will accomplish just as much—and can be less humiliating or resentment-arousing to the worker involved. Most companies still feel, however, that the layoff step is essential in order to convince the worker that management intends to take rule violations seriously.

2. Traditionally, too, when a worker is discharged he is expected to leave the plant immediately, even if he has an appeal in process. Several unions have proposed that—except for the most serious and obvious rule violations—the individual should be allowed to continue to work until his case is finally resolved. This is the practice in a number of government agencies and also in portions of Swedish industry.

3. Here and there workers have won the right to discipline their fellow workers. Workers' self-discipline occurs under union auspices in some parts of the clothing industry. Even the militant National Union of Mineworkers in England has participated on occasion in peer disciplinary programs. One such occasion occurred in a mine which was threatened with close-down because of poor productivity, part of which was caused by high miner absenteeism. The union interviewed over 300 of its members and recommended 40 be dismissed for bad attendance. This and other measures contributed to a doubling of productivity and the saving of the mine.

The standard union position, however, is that discipline is management's function and that the union's role, if any, is to protect the worker involved. Peer discipline, of course, is a well established principle (even if an indifferently achieved practice) in many professions.

4. The growing recognition that alcoholism is a disease has led many companies to re-evaluate their use of discipline to handle cases of drunkenness. Referals to counseling or to such organizations as Alcoholics Anonymous have been employed increasingly as a substitute for traditional discipline.

While each of these innovative approaches to rule enforcement suffers from serious disadvantages which may limit its applicability, as a group they represent attempts to provide workers with greater dignity on the job.

Consideration's Impact on Productivity and Satisfaction

What is consideration's impact on the quality of worklife? Common sense suggests that considerately treated workers are likely to feel more satisfied, but what forms of consideration are most important to which sorts of workers? And does consideration have any impact on productivity?

Impact on satisfaction: Despite the lack of firm evidence, common sense suggest that consideration does lead to satisfaction. However, there are some important differences among workers in what "consideration" means and the kinds of needs it satisfies.

For the dependent worker or the worker brought up in an authoritarian culture, the considerate supervisor may provide a father image or a role model and he may be viewed as someone whom the subordinate may lean upon in time of trouble.

Where the work load is uneven or the supervisor has some discretion in handing out rewards, his reputation for fairness (equity) may be especially important.

For workers with high "related" needs, who are assigned to routine jobs, the activities of the supervisor may facilitate or hinder the development of a friendly cohesive work group (e.g., he can cooperate with or disrupt such activities as pay-check-number pools, birthday parties, after-work parties, and the like). Good social relations are especially important also when the job is anxiety-arousing or high team work is required.

Where the job is either considerably more or considerably less challenging than employees want, the supervisor can at least make himself available to listen to gripes. Where it is less challenging, he can also seek to divert their attention to social activities (see above); where it is too challenging, he can provide encouragement and support.

Where the job requires that the supervisor interact frequently with his subordinates (one aspect of close supervision), it is important that the supervisor be supportive and not socially distant, etc. so as to counteract the oppressive features of the constant interaction. Consideration makes the exercise of power more palatable.

Consideration and productivity: Even common sense makes the relationship between consideration and productivity somewhat uncertain. In general, consideration involves the context in which work occurs, and, therefore, consideration should not be considered a motivator or related to productivity. While there may be no simple relationship between consideration and productivity, some relationships probably do exist. These have been formulated in a number of different fashions (some of which merely represent alternative ways of saying the same thing)—and some of these approaches involve expectancy theory.

1. *Happy workers work harder.* Implicit in the philosophy of paternalism rampant during the 1920s was the assumption that there was a direct relationship between morale and productivity. Decently treated workers would be happier and therefore work harder, possibly out of sheer gratitude. Such a simplistic view of the relationship is no longer in vogue today, nevertheless it is still the unspoken basis of some management rhetoric.

2. *Consideration reduces frustrations and therefore reduces barriers to production.* For unsatisfying tasks, consideration may serve as a "stress reducer," counteracting the oppressive nature of the job.

3. *Consideration is a reward for productivity.* This reward may involve just a simple exchange, or it may serve as one of the considerations in an "implicit bargain."

4. *Consideration may reduce productivity because workers are no longer as afraid of being punished.* This hypothesis, at first glance, is merely another version of the pre-Human Relations philosophy that a supervisor has got to be tough if he is to get the work out. In sharp contrast to previous hypotheses, it suggests that having a highly considerate, easy-going, nonpunitive supervisor may actually inhibit production since subordinates may conclude that he is too nice a person, too much of a good friend to punish them for goofing off.

5. *Consideration may change subordinate values.* More specifically, the supervisor may be able to induce individuals or groups to place higher values (technically: different "valences") on performance as a goal.

6. *Consideration may strengthen the effort-performance relationship.* Put in less fancy terms, this means that consideration may make it easier for workers to get the job done and therefore may increase the perceived relative value of any payoff existing for higher productivity.

7. *Consideration may make the performance-reward relationship seem more equitable.* A boss who is seen as fair will also be seen as handing out rewards in terms of contribution. This will increase the perceived payoff for effort.

A Final Word on Consideration

If nothing else, the above discussion should make it clear that it is difficult to make sweeping statements about either the nature or the impact of consideration. What is viewed as appropriate or considerate depends upon a variety of circumstances—cultural, technical, and organizational—and a contingency approach is required.

It is clear that supervisory consideration does contribute to making a satisfactory work environment and therefore to worker satisfaction—but for some workers and in some situations this is more important than it is for others. Despite the absence of a demonstrated direct relationship between consideration and productivity, consideration may reduce worker frustration and make other motivational approaches more effective. Or, to put it another way, even where the presence of consideration does little to increase productivity, its absence is likely to reduce it.

FACILITATION

"The supervisor has two jobs: he must be concerned with his subordinates and he must get the work out." Accurate as the first part of this statement may be, the second is too simple. The supervisor does not get the work out by himself. Instead he structures the work situations so that others can do the job more effectively.

Facilitation, i.e., the ability to organize work and direct subordinates, may seem a rather humdrum virtue compared with concern for people or ability to foster participation or enthusiasm for organizational goals; nevertheless, the supervisor who wastes his employees' efforts is likely to suffer from not only a poor productivity record, but also a group of frustrated, dissatisified employees whose quality of worklife will be low. This facilitation function may be approached in a number of ways.

Strengthening the Expectancy Relationship: A Check List

How can the supervisor strengthen the path-goal relationship so that employees perceive that increased efforts in fact are rewarded in a manner which provides valued satisfactions? Among the things he can do are the following:

1. He can increase the perceived likelihood that increased effort will lead to performance:
— by providing clear goals, i.e., by indicating the nature of the performance desired.
— by providing guidance, i.e., by teaching and otherwise instructing his subordinates *how* to work for desired goals.
— by providing the tools, supplies, etc. required to do the job.
— by encouraging the development of cohesive work teams.
— by obtaining efficiency-improving suggestions from subordinates through the process of participation.

2. He can increase the perceived likelihood that greater performance will lead to rewards:
— by working with higher management to recast the reward and promotion (career) systems so that rewards and promotions more closely reflect performance.
— by providing rewards of his own (for example, praise) for higher productivity.
— by redesigning jobs in such a fashion that completing a unit of work now becomes a reward in itself.
— by encouraging participation in work decisions.

3. He can increase the feeling that the relationship between performance and rewards is equitable, among other means by monitoring the rewards to insure that (a) they are commensurate with performance, (b) they are distributed equitably, and (c) employees have adequate opportunities to participate in deciding how rewards will be distributed and/or to have their grievances heard when apparent inequities occur.

4. He can increase the value of rewards in terms of satisfaction.

5. He can develop (or influence higher management to develop) adequate methods of feedback so that employees may more accurately perceive the effort-reward relationship.

Establishing Performance Standards

Effort is misused unless it is made clear what the goals are toward which these efforts should be directed. The establishment of goals or performance standards seems to be a necessary, but not sufficient condition for productivity. Under most circumstances clear standards also contribute to satisfaction. Ambiguity and uncertainty merely lead to waste effort and frustration. Concrete goals direct effort, reduce uncertainty, and serve as an instrument of communications.

Performance standards may be qualitative (in terms of what sorts of things to do) or quantitative (in terms of how much to do). They may be set arbitrarily by the boss, through group discussion, or as a result of either explicit or implicit bargaining. New standards may be set every few minutes or on a long-term basis. Regardless of how these standards are set, it is important that subordinates know what they are expected to accomplish.

Some jobs are so routine, of course, that no one has any problem knowing what he is expected to do. Under such circumstances, the supervisor who emphasizes the obvious sounds as if he is nagging. Nevertheless, there are many assignments which may be quite clear to the boss who assigns them, but totally unclear to the subordinate who receives the assignment.

All this may seem so self-evident as not to be worth mentioning, and yet, hard-nosed as managers are supposed to be, many find it difficult to operationalize their goals—to be really specific as to what they want either their subordinates or the work group as a whole to accomplish. Quite frequently employees say "I'm not really sure what the boss wants me to do," or "when I got hired nobody told me what my exact responsibilities were."

Too often supervisors, imbued with the "Human Relations" point of view, will avoid the seeming unpleasantness of making their expectations clear (though they perhaps later crack down without warning on the unsuspecting subordinate when these unspoken expectations are not met). These supervisors recognize that setting and insisting upon high standards sometimes leads to hostility. As one executive put it: "Every organization has to have a bastard to get things done, and I'm the one picked to do it," to which Harry Truman added, "If you can't stand the heat, get out of the kitchen."

Standards, of course, do not have to be set unilaterally by the boss. Many of the quality of worklife experiments have involved group-set production goals, usually within broad limits set by higher management. Among the organizations which have utilized this approach to goal setting has been the R. G. Barry Company. "We got the operators involved in setting goals," its production manager reported, "because we wanted to have individual and company goals the same." A number of instances have been reported in which production levels under group-set standards are considerably higher than when these standards were set by management. Participation of this sort may not be universally appropriate, however, and later on some of the conditions under which it may or may not work will be suggested.

Management by Objectives (MBO) is an example of participatory goal setting on a managerial level. MBO involves (1) the setting of concrete goals for each manager, (2) on a participatory basis, usually through discussion between the manager and his boss. Among the advantages of MBO (at least when it works as it should) are that it requires management to define exactly what it wants to accomplish and specify all important objectives, especially those commonly ignored (such as employee development); it forces the development of a plan which tells each manager exactly what he is expected to accomplish during the next evaluation period. MBO includes a strong element of participation, yet the evidence suggests that it is the setting of concrete goals, not the participation, which makes the critical difference in productivity and morale. There is no essential reason why MBO might not be applied at the worker level, at least on a modified basis.

Standards can be set Harry-Truman-like by the boss, on an autonomous basis by the work group, or jointly by boss and subordinate (as in MBO). The important thing is that they be set, that people know what they are expected to do.

Three final comments as to standards and their use:

1. High standards contribute to both productivity and satisfaction. Reaching a tough goal—as long as it is fair and reasonable—provides more of a sense of achievement than does reaching an easy goal. History, our every day observations, and research all tell us that the inspiring, respected leader is the one who urges on his men to the very limits of their capabilities. This was Vince Lombardi's secret.

2. Short-run standards are generally more motivating than long-run standards (provided the period is not too short). Finishing a chapter in an hour is usually a more compelling goal than reading a long book over a weekend. By breaking the work down into units or batches, management can give the employee a feeling of completion every time he completes a batch. The desire to finish a unit has strong "pulling power" and also enhances the worker's efficiency.

3. Standards are generally motivating if frequent feedback is provided. All of us like to know how we are doing; lack of such knowledge can be very frustrating. Feedback can be motivating, as the following story illustrates:

> In a plant that manufactures a large number of small items at high speed, management installed counters on each of the production lines, just for supervisory purposes. Soon the employees were spending so much time sneaking a look that additional counters were installed

at each work place. Informal competition developed both between lines and between shifts at each work place. Then the foreman brought in a blackboard and the men began posting their records, thus increasing the spirit of competition.

Guiding employee efforts: The employee wants to know not just what to accomplish but also how to accomplish it. Without appropriate training or instruction, the subordinate's efforts are wasted and both productivity and satisfaction suffer.

The supervisor can provide guidance to his subordinates in a variety of ways, among others, the following:

— He can supervise them closely on a minute-by-minute basis, telling them exactly what to do.
— He can provide detailed advance instructions (rules) covering most likely contingencies.
— He can make himself available for subordinates' questions, but otherwise let them work things out by themselves.
— He can provide broad forms of training which impart appropriate skills.

Typically, the supervisor will use a combination of the above techniques. However, the particular mixture used in any given situation has considerable implications for the quality of worklife. The supervisor who supervises on a minute-by-minute basis is normally felt to be supervising more closely than the one who emphasizes training or is merely available to provide help when asked.

How close should such guidance be? The answer seems to depend on the nature of the job, on the subordinate's previous training and skills, and to some extent on his personality and orientation toward work. Insufficient guidance can be frustrating and can lead to wasted work efforts, thus reducing both satisfaction and productivity (however, forcing people to solve problems by themselves often provides a useful learning experience). On the other hand, too close supervision is felt as being restrictive (and as indicating lack of consideration), and thus sometimes leads to reduced productivity and to heightened resistance to change.

On routine work, it is relatively easy to provide over-supervision, and it is chiefly on routine work that evidence has been collected associating close supervision with low productivity and dissatisfaction. On nonroutine work rather close supervision may be viewed as helpful.

Oversupervision can be particularly frustrating for employees who have a high growth need and who are expressively oriented toward their jobs. Such workers want a fair amount of freedom to develop their own approaches to work group problems, and perceived close control may be particularly threatening to their egos. On the other hand, instrumentally oriented workers and those with low growth needs may be somewhat more tolerant of the closely supervising boss, provided he adheres to the civilities of consideration. In fact, for some highly dependent employees close supervision may be viewed as providing security and a sign that their boss is interested in them as individuals.

On some sorts of work close coordination is required. Such coordination may be provided either by the members of the group themselves (as in a string quartet), or by the boss himself (as in a symphony orchestra) acting as a close supervisor. Failure to provide such coordination lowers both satisfaction and quality of product.

One last point here: for the supervisor to provide effective guidance he must be viewed as technically competent. As indicated earlier, "having a technically competent supervisor" ranked high among factors correlated to overall job satisfaction. Competence is especially important, of course, where the work is technical or the nature of the job is rapidly changing. Technical skill is even more critical in certain types of endeavor where close coordination is required between members of the work team—as in flying a plane, conducting an orchestra, or operating on a patient.

The technically competent supervisor is not only able to provide more effective guidance to his subordinates, but the mere fact of his competence increases their respect for him and provides him legitimacy as a supervisor. Indeed subordinates often subject a new supervisor to a period of testing and initiation to determine whether he measures up to their standards. This feeling that the boss should show technical skills is particularly strong among men who take pride in their work and closely identify with their occupation (building tradesmen or pilots, for example).

Providing technical support: Even the most highly motivated worker finds it hard to get his work done without adequate tools or supplies, when he has difficulty coordinating his efforts with other workers, or when he has insufficient information to get the job done. Obviously one of the most critical of the supervisor's functions is his ability to provide his subordinates with the wherewithall to accomplish their jobs.

The importance of this function is underscored by the previously mentioned Michigan survey in which "I receive enough help and equipment to get the job done" was ranked "very important" by more employees (69 per cent) than any other item on a long list.

Technical support of the type mentioned above often depends heavily on the supervisor's ability to build good working relations with his own superiors, with staff groups, and with other departments. Organizing effective liaison relations of this sort requires time. It also requires substantial top management support. At times, the supervisor's ability to develop effective relations outside his department may be as critical for employee satisfaction and productivity as anything he does within the department.

Increasing satisfaction gained from productivity: For most workers completing the job well provides some sense of satisfaction. However, the value of this reward (as some say, its "valence") may be increased if the job itself is seen as significant. Work that seems purposeless is bound to lead to frustration. One of the most unpleasant forms of punishment used by the military is to have men dig holes and fill them in again. On the other hand, telephone supervisors report that production and morale are always higher during an emergency. As one said, "It's amazing. An operator may be a low producer and a disciplinary problem, often tardy and absent, but come a blizzard when highways are closed, she will walk long distances to come to work."

Thus anything the supervisor can do to increase the satisfaction gained from completing the job will also strengthen the expectancy relationship. And one way to enhance the worker's sense of achievement is to stress the social value of the product being made, for example in relieving suffering, in advancing organizational objectives, or just accomplishing organizational objectives. This is a common approach to motivation in China and Cuba and is used by almost every country in time of war. It works best where the individual (or group) already strongly identifies with the organizational objectives, for instance in some hospitals or educational institutions. Nevertheless, a certain amount of pride and organizational identification is possible in amost any organization, provided that the basic aspects of consideration are available, and provided that, for expressively oriented individuals with growth needs, there are some meaningful opportunities to do challenging work.

Reward Systems

The material in this chapter is based on "Improving the Quality of Worklife Reward Systems," prepared for the Assistant Secretary for Planning, Evaluation and Research, U.S. Department of Labor, by Edward E. Lawler, III, the University of Michigan and published as PB 255 045, June 1975.

One of the most salient and important attributes of work organizations is their ability to give rewards. Organizations distribute a large number of significant rewards to their members every day. Pay, promotions, fringe benefits, and status symbols are perhaps the most important but certainly not all of the important rewards which are distributed. Because these rewards are important, the way they are distributed has a profound effect on the quality of worklife that employees experience as well as on the effectiveness of organizations.

Despite the obvious importance of rewards in organization, most of the writings concerned with quality of worklife have tended to ignore or down play their importance. This is a serious oversight and one that needs to be corrected if organizations are to be designed in ways that provide a high quality of worklife. Research shows that some rewards contribute more than others to a high quality of worklife, and that some approaches to reward distribution contribute more to a high quality of worklife than others. Before reviewing the characteristics of different rewards and some of the approaches to reward system design, it is necessary to review briefly what is known about what determines people's reactions to rewards.

REWARD SYSTEMS AND INDIVIDUAL SATISFACTION

A great deal of research has been done on what determines whether an individual will be satisfied with the rewards he or she receives from a situation. Despite what common sense might lead one to predict, satisfaction is not a simple function of how much is received. In fact, it is a rather complex reaction to a situation, and it is influenced by a number of factors. Five conclusions can be reached about what determines satisfaction with rewards.

Satisfaction with a reward is a function of both how much is received and how much the individual feels should be received: Most theories of satisfaction stress that people's feelings about how satisfied they are with the amount of a reward they receive are determined by a comparison between what they receive and what they feel they should receive or would like to receive. When individuals receive less than they feel they should receive, they are dissatisfied. When they receive more than they feel they should, they tend to feel guilty and uncomfortable. Feelings of overreward seem to be easily overcome by individuals and are therefore rather infrequent (surveys show that only about five percent of the people feel that they are overpaid). These feelings are overcome by a change in the way an individual perceives the situation, for instance, by an increase in his perception of his own worth. It is more difficult to remove a feeling of underreward; this can sometimes be accomplished only by an actual change in the situation (e.g., higher pay or a new job).

It is because individuals have feelings about what they should receive that individuals who receive less of a given reward often are more satisfied with the amount of the reward they have received than are those who receive more. For example, people who are highly paid in comparison to others doing the same jobs often are more satisifed than are individuals who are much higher paid but are poorly paid in comparison to others doing the same kind of job.

People's feelings of satisfaction are influenced by comparisons with what happens to others: People's feelings are very much influenced by what happens to people who are like themselves. They seem to compare what others do and what they receive with their own situation. These comparisons are made both inside and outside the organizations they work in, but they are usually made with similar people. Based upon this comparison, they reach conclusions about what rewards they should receive. When the overall comparison between their situation and that of others is favorable, they tend to be satisfied. People consider such inputs as their education, training, seniority, job performance and the nature of their jobs when they think about the rewards and what they should be.

People differ substantially in which inputs they think should be most important in determining their rewards. Typically they believe that the inputs in which they excel should be weighed the most highly. This, of course, means that it is very difficult to have everyone satisfied with their rewards, since people tend to make their comparisons based on what is most favorable to them. Individuals also tend to rate their inputs higher than do others. Still, it is possible to influence how satisfied employees are by altering the total amount of rewards that are given and by altering how they are distributed. Some distribution patterns clearly are seen as more equitable, since they are more closely related to the inputs of individuals and therefore to what people feel they should receive.

Overall job satisfaction is influenced by how satisfied employees are with both the intrinsic and extrinsic rewards they receive from their jobs: In addition to the obvious extrinsic rewards individuals receive (e.g., pay, promotion, status symbols), they also may experience internal feelings that are rewarding to them. These include feelings of competence, achievement, personal growth, and self esteem. The overall job satisfaction of most people is determined both by how they feel about their intrinsic rewards and how they feel about their extrinsic rewards.

A number of writers have debated the issue of whether extrinsic rewards are more important than intrinsic rewards in determining job satisfaction. No study has yet been done that definitely establishes one as more important than the other; most show that both are very important and have a substantial impact on overall satisfaction. It seems quite clear also that they cannot be directly substituted for each other since they satisfy different needs. Consequently, money will not make up for a boring repetitive job—just as an interesting job will not make up for low pay.

People differ widely in the rewards they desire and in how important the different rewards are to them: Probably the most frequently and hotly debated topic in this area concerns how important the different rewards are to employees. One group says money is the most important, another says interesting work is. Both groups, of course, are able to find examples to support their point of view, since for some people money is most important while for others job content is the most important. People differ substantially and in meaningful ways in what is important to them.

Overall, how reward systems operate seems to have a bigger influence on individuals' satisfaction with rewards than on the importance people attach to rewards. Both of these can be influenced by the amount of rewards which organizations give but the first seems to be much more susceptible to influence, since it is directly influenced by reward levels. The importance of rewards is influenced by things which are beyond the control of organizations (e.g., family background, the economic climate) as well as by satisfaction.

Many extrinsic rewards are important and satisfying only because they lead to other rewards: There is nothing inherently valuable about many of the things which people seek in organizations. They are important only because they lead to other things or because of their symbolic value. A certain kind of desk or office, for example, often is seen as a reward because it is indicative of power and status. Money is important to some people only because it produces other attractive things—goods, status, etc. If money did not lead to such things it would decrease in importance.

Because extrinsic rewards lead to other rewards, they can satisfy many needs and thus remain important even when conditions change. The ability of extrinsic rewards to satisfy many needs also helps to make reward systems difficult to design and administer in a way that will produce a high quality of worklife.

Necessary Reward System Properties

Based upon what has been said so far about rewards and satisfaction, we can identify some properties that any reward system in an organization must have if it is to produce a high quality of work-life.

First, it must make enough rewards available so that individuals' basic needs are satisfied. Basic needs for food, shelter, safety and existence must be met before external comparisons become relevant. If they are not met, job satisfaction will not exist even if external comparisons are favorable. Fortunately, in most work situations, these needs are met as a result of federal legislation and union agreements. However, the need for job security is often lacking despite the efforts of government and unions. Just meeting basic needs is not enough in most situations, however. Unless the reward levels compare favorably with what other organizations do, individuals will not be satisfied with their rewards because they will inevitably note that they are not as well off as others.

Secondly, the rewards that are available must be distributed in a way that is seen as equitable by the people in the organization. People compare their situation with that of people both inside and outside the organization. They are likely to be dissatisfied if people in their organization whom they perceive as less deserving receive more rewards, even though they themselves are in a good position with respect to the outside market. Most people have a sense of equity, and this involves considerations of how much they receive in comparison to others around them, regardless of the absolute amount they receive and their position in the outside market. In order to construct a system that is high in internal (within organization) equity, it is necessary to base it on the perceptions of the people who are in the organization. The most direct way to take their perceptions into account is to have them make the decision about how much they will be rewarded.

Finally, the reward system must deal with organization members as individuals. This means recognizing their individuality by giving them the kind of rewards they desire. This point is crucial because of the large differences among individuals in what they want. Unless these are explicitly recognized, it is unlikely that a reward system will be broad enough and flexible to encompass the range of individual differences which exist.

REWARD SYSTEMS AND ORGANIZATIONAL EFFECTIVE-NESS

In looking at the role of rewards in organizations it is not enough to look only at their impact on the quality of worklife. Consideration must also be given to their impact on organizational effectiveness. They play such a vital role in influencing organizational effectiveness that to ignore this is to deny an important aspect of organizational reality. The actual adoption of any reward system hinges at least partially upon the impact it is expected to have on organizational effectiveness. No reward system which substantially reduces organizational effectiveness is likely to be voluntarily adopted no matter how much it contributes to a high quality of worklife. The challenge is to find reward systems which contribute to both organizational effectiveness and the quality of worklife.

Organizations typically rely on reward systems to do four things: (1) motivate employees to perform effectively, (2) motivate employees to join the organization, (3) motivate employees to come to work, and (4) reinforce the organizational structure by indicating the position of different individuals in the organizations.

Reward Systems and Motivation

There is no question that reward systems can and do influence how motivated individuals are to perform their jobs effectively. When certain specifiable conditions exist, reward systems motivate performance. What are those conditions? Basically, important rewards must be perceived to be tied in timely fashion to effective performance. Stated another way, the research shows that organizations get the kind of behavior that is seen to lead to the rewards employees value. In many ways this is a deceptively simple statement of the conditions which must exist if rewards are to motivate performance. A good measure of performance, the ability to identify the kinds of rewards which are important to particular individuals, and the ability to control the amount of the rewards received by a specific individual—all these factors are important, and none is easy to accomplish in most organizational settings.

Organizations must not only tie important rewards to performance, but must do so in a way which makes evident the connection. In addition, a climate of trust and credibility must exist in the organization so that employees can believe that good performance will lead to desirable rewards.

Reward Systems and Organizational Membership

There is a great deal of evidence that shows that the kinds of rewards an organization offers directly influence the decisions people make about whether to initially join the organization and their decision about when and if to quit. All other things being equal, individuals tend to gravitate toward and remain in those organizations that give the greatest rewards. A large number of studies have found that turnover is strongly related to job satisfaction and somewhat less strongly to satisfaction with the extrinsic rewards a person receives. Apparently this comes about because individuals who are presently satisifed with their jobs expect to continue to be satisfied and as a result want to stay with the same organization.

The objective, then, is to design a reward system that is effective at retaining the best employees. To do this, a reward system must distribute rewards in a way that will lead to a feeling of satisfaction by the better performers when they compare their rewards with those received by individuals in other organizations. The emphasis here, then, is on external comparisons, because turnover means leaving an organization for a better situation elsewhere. One way to accomplish this, of course, is to reward everyone at a level that is above what exists in other organizations. This strategy has two drawbacks. In the case of some rewards (e.g., money), it is very costly. It also can cause feelings of intra-organizational inequity, because better performers feel inequitably treated when they are rewarded at the same level as poor performers even though they are fairly treated in terms of external comparisons. Faced with this situation the better performers may not quit, but they are likely to be dissatisfied, complain, look for internal transfers, and mistrust the organization.

What, then, is the best solution? It would seem to be to have competitive reward levels and to base rewards on performance. This should lead to the better performers being satisfied and staying with the organization. It is important to note, however, that not only must the better performers be treated better than the poor performers; they must be treated significantly better because they feel they deserve more. Otherwise, they will still feel they are not properly rewarded and eventually leave the organization.

In summary, managing turnover means managing satisfaction. This depends on effectively relating rewards to performance, something that is often difficult to do. When it cannot be accomplished, about all an organization can do is to try to reward individuals at an above-average level. In situations where turnover is costly, this should be an effective strategy even if it involves giving out expensive rewards.

Organizational Effectiveness and Absenteeism

A great deal of research has shown that absenteeism and satisfaction are related. As would be expected, when people are satisfied with their jobs, they come to work regularly. Thus, attendance at work, like membership in an organization, is a function of the rewards that come with it. When work is a pleasant rewarding place to be, individuals come regularly; when it isn't, they don't because they prefer to be elsewhere.

High absenteeism, like turnover, is expensive. Like its twin, tardiness, it leads to a need for over staffing and often leads to untrained and inexperienced individuals doing jobs. Thus, it makes sense for organizations to adopt reward policies which reduce absenteeism. What kind of reward policies will do this? Basically, reward policies that make work a satisfying place to be and which tie rewards to attendance. With respect to the latter point, several studies have shown that by tying pay bonuses and other rewards to attendance, absenteeism can be reduced. This approach is costly, but sometimes it is less costly than absenteeism. It seems to be a particularly useful strategy in situations where the work itself and the working conditions are poor and do not lend themselves to meaningful improvements. In situations where these conditions can be changed, changing them often is the most effective and cost efficient way to deal with absenteeism.

Reward Systems and Organizational Structure

One of the characteristics of all complex organizations is that a division of labor exists. This, in turn, leads to a differentiated and hierarchical structure. Organizations do differ, however, in the degree to which members have unique, highly specialized jobs, and in the degree of hierarchical differentiation which exists. Some organizations, for example, are characterized by relatively flat structures and only a few levels of management, while others have many levels (often as many as 20 in the case of large organizations). Some organizations are broken up into many departments, each of which has a function, while others as a matter of policy try to discourage a high level of functional specialization.

There has been a continuing debate over what type of organization structure and indeed what kind of managerial style is most effective. At this point in time, the evidence tends to suggest that no one structure is always best. It seems to depend on such things as the type of product which is being produced or the type of service which is being delivered, the type of external environment the firm is trying to operate in, and the type of people who are in the organization.

It does seem that regardless of the organization structure used, the reward systems in organizations should always be congruent with it. One way a reward system can be congruent with the structure of an organization is in the degree to which it serves to differentiate among organization members based upon their formal position in the organization. The military is perhaps the clearest example of an organization which very effectively uses the reward system to differentiate between people in different positions. Each rank has different privileges down to the point of separate officer clubs and housing areas on bases. The argument in favor of this is that it helps make the organization more effective because it clearly establishes who has authority and it makes it easier for subordinates to take orders because they are taking them from the position rather than the person.

At the other extreme are organizations which consciously try to give everyone the same fringe benefits, parking spaces, and offices in order to diminish the distance between different levels in the organization. The argument here is that not differentiating among people in terms of rewards and symbols of office, when combined with a relatively flat organization structure, produces an organization that is highly participative, equalitarian, and flexible. The further argument is that large differences between people in a more participative organization are incongruent with this style of management and organization structure and would be counter-productive.

A second area in which reward systems may or may not be congruent with the management style and structure of an organization concerns decision making. Organizations differ significantly in the degree to which decisions are made in a centralized hierarchical manner. In some they are concentrated at the top, in others they are made at the lowest possible level. In terms of reward systems, congruence requires that decisions about reward allocations be made in the same manner as other important decisions.

CHARACTERISTICS OF EXTRINSIC REWARDS

There are at least five identifiable characteristics which rewards should have if they are to contribute optimally to a high quality of worklife and organizational effectiveness. These are importance, flexibility, frequency with respect to administration, visibility, and low cost.

A reward must be important to some individual or group of individuals if it is to influence organizational effectiveness and employee satisfaction. Thus, the first question that needs to be asked about any reward is whether it is, in fact, a valued reward to the particular individuals involved.

A reward system which relies solely on generally important rewards inevitably is going to miss some employees, because even rewards which are important to most employees are not important to all. This creates the need for individualizing rewards so that each employee will receive the reward he or she desires. In some situations, individualization can be accomplished and the quality of worklife improved by giving people the choice of which extrinsic rewards they will receive. For example, one company allows workers who have finished their daily production quota the chance of either going home or receiving extra pay. If rewards are to be tailored to individuals, they must be flexible both with respect to the amount given and whether they are given to each person in the organization. It is impossible to create individualized reward packages without flexibility. It is also impossible equitably to vary rewards according to the performance of individuals.

Clearly related to the issue of flexibility is the issue of how frequently rewards can be given. Giving rewards frequently is often necessary to sustain extrinsic motivation and satisfaction. The best rewards, then, can be given frequently without losing their importance.

The visibility of rewards is important because it influences the ability of the reward to satisfy esteem and recognition needs. Low visibility rewards cannot satisfy these needs and therefore often are less important. Visibility is also important in helping make clear the relationship between rewards and performance.

Finally, the cost of the reward is relevant because it is a constraint in organizations that must be considered. A high cost reward simply cannot be given as often and when used reduces organizational effectiveness as a result of its cost.

Table 4.1 presents an evaluation of the common rewards which are used by organizations in terms of their average importance, flexibility, visibility, frequency, and cost. As can be seen from the table, none of the rewards rate highly on all of the criteria. Interestingly, pay seems to possess all the characteristics necessary to make it the perfect extrinsic reward except one—that of low cost. It is particularly expensive to use as an extrinsic reward, since individuals need to receive frequent pay increases or bonuses in order for sustained extrinsic motivation and satisfaction to be present.

Promotion, dismissal, and tenure are all low in flexibility. They simply cannot be easily varied in amount as the situation calls for. They also cannot be given very regularly. This makes it very difficult to tie them closely to performance over a long period of time. Job tenure or a guarantee of permanent employment, for example, is a one-shot reward that once given loses all ability to motivate. These rewards also tend to be rather expensive. Their high cost is not as visible and obvious as is the cost of pay but it is nonetheless

TABLE 4.1: AN EVALUATION OF EXTRINSIC REWARDS

	Average Importance	Flexibility in Amount	Visibility	Frequency	Dollar Cost
Pay	High	High	Potentially High	High	High
Promotion	High	Low	High	Low	High
Dismissal	High	Low	High	Low	High
Job Tenure	Moderate	Low	High	Low	High
Status Symbols	Moderate	High	High	Low	Moderate
Special Awards, Certificates and Medals	Low	High	Low	Low	Low
Fringe Benefits	Moderate	Moderate	Moderate	Low	High

real. Special awards, certificates, and medals are examples of rewards with a quite different set of characteristics. They are high in flexibility and visibility. However, they can only be given a few times before they lose their value, and many people do not value them, so that their average importance is relatively low.

In summary, there is no one reward or class of rewards that meets all the criteria for being a good extrinsic reward. Furthermore, organizations have little control over how important different rewards are to individuals. Organizations do control, however, which rewards they use, and it is important that they carefully diagnose the situation and use those which are right for the situation. Failure to do this assures that the reward systems in an organization will not contribute to a high quality of worklife and organizational effectiveness. Table 4.1 points out that promotion, fringe benefits, and pay are probably the extrinsic rewards which have the greatest potential impact on the quality of worklife and organizational effectiveness, since they are important to most individuals. Each of them also has other characteristics which make them potentially effective.

REWARD SYSTEMS AND ORGANIZATION CHANGE

A number of studies indicate an apparent relationship between participation in pay system design and trust. This has some interesting implications for organization change efforts. Many organization change theorists argue that participation can increase trust and satisfaction (see Chapters 9 and 10 for a detailed discussion of participative management), but few suggest that participation start in (or even include) the reward systems of the organization. A recent review of participative management by the International Labor Organization fails to note any examples where participation has included pay system design or administration. In most writings on organization change, pay administration is usually seen as a difficult area to work in and one that is to be dealt with only after a spirit of trust and participation has been established.

Certainly one cannot disagree with the point that pay and rewards can be handled after a spirit of trust and participation has been established. However, the possibility of starting organization development efforts with participation in pay administration—precisely because it is so important and difficult to deal with—should not be overlooked. An alternative is to begin with some other rewards (e.g., promotion). There are reasons for favoring pay, however, since, as already noted, it is important to most people. Moreover, there are a number of interesting and significant changes which can be made that have the potential of improving the quality of worklife and organizational effectiveness.

The idea of starting an organization development program with changes in pay system decision making is consistent with the literature which suggests that participation is likely to be meaningful only when it involves decisions that are important to employees, on which they have information, and in which they want to participate. It also seems likely to lead to organization-wide changes because of the importance of the pay area and because pay changes affect all levels in an organization. This is in notable contrast to some other approaches (e.g., job redesign) which start with small groups and often have trouble spreading to the rest of the organization. Success here can strongly reinforce a more participative style of management, and thus, lead to experimentation with other issues. Pay system changes are also highly visible and immediate in organizations and, as such, can produce rapid change.

In order to design an adequate pay system (particularly an incentive system), employees have to have a good idea of how their organization operates from an economic point of view. This requires some education but it often pays dividends since this knowledge can help the employees do their jobs better and can lead to their making valuable suggestions.

Even if an organization doesn't want to begin by using participation in the pay area, pay system changes can be helpful in establishing the significance of an organization change project. Putting everyone on salary, for example, can communicate that things are different. Doing an attitude survey and adjusting the pay system according to the results can communicate to employees that the organization is concerned about their preferences. Starting a job redesign change effort by giving everyone a pay increase so that they are paid for their new job before they are doing it can be a way of indicating that individuals will be doing more important jobs and that the change is for real.

A strong case can be made for the point that an organization should always consider the reward system implications of an organizational change project before it begins the project. Often organizations begin projects without thinking about pay or by simply saying that pay system problems will be worked out later. For example, a number of organizations that have gone into job enrichment projects have said that a gains sharing system will be worked out later if gains materialize. The advisability of this approach is doubtful. A good guess, and it is only a guess at this time, is that it is easier to work out a gain sharing plan before there is anything to share than it is after there is a fixed amount available. It would seem that waiting until the gains have materialized is more likely to create a dysfunctional bargaining situation.

Organizations also have been known to give pay increases to employees in job enrichment experiments without considering the effect on other employees. Even though the other employees are not adversely affected, they still often feel inequitably treated. In some cases this has led to their demanding that either they be allowed to participate in the project or that it be cancelled. This kind of pressure can be functional since it can encourage dissemination, but it can also be dysfunctional if dissemination is difficult or premature.

SYSTEM CONGRUENCE

A case can be made for the view that the spread of participation from pay to other areas of decision making is not only a logical consequence of its success in the pay area, but a necessary one if the pay system is to continue to work well. One important determinant of how well the reward system in an organization operates may well be the congruence between how it and the other systems in the organization are run or designed. It is frequently pointed out in the literature on organization structure that organizations have multiple systems; it is less often pointed out that in order to have an effective organization, all the systems must be congruous.

The reason for this is that when incongruence exists, a role conflict situation is set up, and employees receive conflicting messages about what behavior is expected of them and how the organization regards them. Although employees are capable of a certain degree of compartmentalization, it is difficult and uncomfortable for them to have the area of rewards isolated from other organizational areas for a long time.

Systems usually head toward balance and this often leads them to reject the changes which have been introduced, unless they are part of a total system change. One implication of this is that changes which start with the reward system must spread to other areas; another is that changes which start elsewhere must before too long deal with the reward system so that congruence will exist.

It would seem that congruence must exist within and between two areas: decision making process and system design or structure. As far as the decision making process is concerned, congruence would seem to mean that decisions about such things as rate of production, product quality, new employee selection, and purchasing are made in the same way as decisions about rewards. As far as design or structure is concerned, congruence would mean that the type of job evaluation plan (e.g., skill bonus vs. point method) and the type of incentive plan which is used (e.g., group, individual) are supportive in a measurement and reward sense with the way jobs are designed and decisions are made. Specifically, the reward system needs to measure and reward those things that are critical in making the job and organization design work (e.g., cooperation, skill acquisition), and it needs to measure behavior at the same level (e.g., individual, group or department) as the job design emphasizes. It also would seem to mean that the reward system should emphasize those differences among people which are supportive of the basic structure and decision making approach in the organization.

The importance of congruence has often been overlooked by people who take job enrichment and participative management approaches to organization development. There are a number of cases where either a traditional job enrichment approach was tried or an autonomous work group approach was tried, and nothing was done to change the structure of the reward system. The result in almost every instance was problems caused by a misfit between the structural design of the pay system and the new job designs. For example, in several instances job enrichment and job rotation were done, but a traditional job evaluation was left in place. This resulted in employee demands for higher pay because they now had more responsibility. Management had trouble answering these demands because the job evaluation was designed for situations where employees did not rotate and acquire new skills. And in one plant, a woman who was asked to take notes at team meetings asked for a raise because she had taken on secretarial duties.

In another case, a large airline tried an autonomous work group experiment with its maintenance employees that failed because the pay system was not changed. The employees were not on an incentive plan, but they had, over the years, come to expect large amounts of overtime. In effect, since harder work didn't get them more money and slow work did (it got overtime), they had decided to work overtime in order to earn more money. Establishment of an autonomous work group in this instance did not increase performance because it was against the best economic interests of the employees.

All this suggests some interesting conclusions about what constitutes congruence between certain processes and structural areas in organizations. Table 4.2 shows what type of reward system practices are congruent with a more traditional or authoritative approach to organization design and management (theory X in McGregor's terminology) and which are more congruent with a more human resources or participative oriented approach (theory Y). By a traditional approach is meant such things as strict specialization and standardization of function, and a tall organization structure with a strict hierarchical approach to decision making. By a more human resource approach is meant management that is based upon pushing decision making down to lower levels, an emphasis on creating meaningful jobs, a flat organization and an emphasis on openness within the organization.

Neither of these approaches is necessarily superior to the other. According to the theory, it all depends on the type of environment which is being dealt with and the type of technology employed. Thus, we cannot conclude that one style of reward and adminis-

TABLE 4.2: APPROPRIATE REWARD SYSTEMS PRACTICES

Reward System	Traditional or Theory X	Participative or Theory Y
Fringe Benefits	Vary according to organization level	Cafeteria—same for all levels
Promotion	All decisions made by top management	Open posting for all jobs; peer group involvement in decision process
Status Symbols	A great many carefully allocated on the basis of job position	Few present, low emphasis on organization level
Pay		
Type of System	Hourly and salary	All salary
Base Rate	Based on job performed. High enough to attract job applicants	Based on skills high enough to provide security and attract applicants
Incentive Plan	Piece rate	Group and organization wide bonus, lump sum increase
Communication Policy	Very restricted distribution of information	Individual rates, salary survey data, all other information made public
Decision Making Locus	Top management	Close to location of person whose pay is being set

tration is best. Rather, we must conclude that congruence is always best and that participative decision making with respect to pay, openness about pay, group and plant wide incentives, all salary pay plans, openness about promotion, participation in promotion decisions, cafeteria style fringe benefit plans, and skill based bonus plans are congruent with those new approaches to organization design that emphasize autonomous work groups and job enrichment. We can also conclude that standard job evaluation plans, piece rate incentive or no incentive at all, many status symbols, low openness about promotion and pay decisions, the use of an hourly pay system, and little participation with respect to promotion and pay decisions are congruent with the more traditional top down approach to management.

AN OVERVIEW ON REWARDS

If there is one message here it is that there are reward system practices which can contribute to a high quality of worklife. True, there are no ideal practices, no universal "goods," but there are better and worse practices. Admittedly, what is good and what is bad depends partially on organizational and environmental conditions, but these can be identified and dealt with. On the one hand it seems clear that improving the quality of worklife is not simply a matter of more extrinsic rewards, as some would have us believe. On the other hand, it seems clear that reward systems cannot be ignored in efforts to produce a high quality of worklife.

Table 4.3 summarizes the effect of various reward system practices and processes. Each of the practices is rated on six dimensions. The first three are dimensions that contribute to a high quality of worklife, and the next three are dimensions that contribute to organizational effectiveness. Since these are "new" practices, the question that concerns us is whether they represent improvements over traditional practice (e.g., secrecy versus openness). Thus, each practice is rated on five point scales running from 0 to 4. A "0" indicates that the practice leads to a negligible increase over what is usually present in organizations. A "4" indicates that the practice produces a large increase over what is usually present. One note of caution is in order in interpreting these figures. They should be viewed as averages across all situations. They obviously may not be applicable to any particular situation because of the many factors which condition their validity. Further, they represent the opinions of the author and are supported by little research.

TABLE 4.3: EVALUATION OF REWARD PRACTICES

Reward Practice	External Equity	Internal Equity	Individuality	Performance Motivation	Membership	Absenteeism
Open promotion and job posting	1	3	0	2	2	1
Participation in promotion de-cisions	1	4	0	2	2	1
Cafeteria fringe benefits	2	0	4	0	2	1
Skill based evaluation plans	0	2	3	2	2	2
All salary plans	2	0	1	0	1	0
Lump-sum salary increase plans	0	0	3	1	2	1
Performance pay plans	2	2	3	3	1	1
Scanlon plan	2	0	0	2	2	1
Variable ratio plans	0	0	0	0	0	0
Open pay	1	2	0	2	0	1
Participation in decisions	1	2	0	2	1	1

The ratings suggest that improvements can be obtained both by changing the process and changing the mechanics of reward administration. The process changes that move to a more open and participative system are all rated favorably. The one practice that seems to offer little is variable ratio reward plans. All the others seem to have something to contribute to both a high quality work-life and organizational effectiveness.

Work Redesign—
What Is It? What Does It Do?

The material in this chapter is based on "Improving the Quality of Worklife Design," prepared for the U.S. Department of Labor by J. Richard Hackman, Yale University, and published as PB 255 044, June 1975; and on "Improving the Quality of Worklife . . . and in the Process, Improving Productivity," prepared for the Manpower Administration, U.S. Department of Labor, by Edward M. Glaser, Human Interaction Institute, and published as PB 236 209, August, 1974.

Will the redesign of work evolve into a robust and powerful strategy for organizational change—or will it, like so many of its behavioral science predecessors, fade into disuse as practitioners experience failure and disillusionment in its use? The answer is by no means clear.

Existing evidence regarding the merits of work redesign can be viewed as either optimistic or pessimistic, depending on the biases of the reader. On the one hand, numerous case studies of successful work redesign projects have been published which show that work redesign can be an effective tool for improving both the quality of the work experience of employees and their on-the-job productivity. Yet it also is true that numerous failures in implementing work redesign have been experienced by organizations around the country—and the rate of failure shows no sign of diminishing.

What is Work Redesign?

Obviously any time a job is changed—whether because of a new machine, an internal re-organization, or a whim of a manager—it can be said that "work redesign" has taken place. The present use of the term is somewhat more specialized. Work redesign here refers to any activities that involve the alteration of specific jobs (or interdependent systems of jobs) with the intent of increasing both the quality of the work experience of employees and their on-the-job productivity. The term is deliberately broad, to include the great diversity of changes that can be tried to achieve these goals. It subsumes such terms as "job rotation," "job enrichment," and "socio-technical systems design," each of which refers to a specific approach to or technique for redesigning work.

There are no simple or generally-accepted criteria for a well-designed job, nor is there any single technology that is acknowledged as the proper way to go about improving a job. Instead, what will be effective for one specific job in a particular organization may be quite different from what should be done in another setting. There are, nonetheless, some things which most work redesign experiments carried out to date have in common. Typically changes are made that provide employees with additional responsibilities for planning, setting up and checking their own work; for making decisions about methods and procedures; for establishing their own work pace within broad limits; and sometimes for relating directly to the client who receives the results of the work. Often the net effect is that jobs which previously had been simplified and segmented into many small parts (in the interest of "efficiency" from an engineering perspective) are simply put back together again and made the responsibility of individual workers.

An early case of work redesign is illustrative. The basic job involved the assembly of a small centrifugal pump used in washing machines. Prior to redesign, the pumps were assembled by six operators on a conveyor line, with each operator performing a particular part of the assembly. The job was changed so that each worker assembled an entire pump, inspected it, and placed his own identifying mark on the pump. In addition, the assembly operations were converted to a "batch" system in which workers had more freedom to control their work pace than had been the case under the conveyor system. Kilbridge reports that after the job had been enlarged, total assembly time decreased, quality improved, and important cost savings were realized.

In another case, the responsibilities of clerks who helped assemble information for telephone directories at Indiana Bell Telephone were significantly expanded. Prior to the change, a "production line" model was used to assemble directory information: information was passed from clerk to clerk as it was processed, with each clerk performing only a very small part of the entire job. There were a total of 21 different steps in the workflow. Jobs were changed so that each qualified clerk was given responsibility for all the clerical operations required to assemble an entire directory—including receiving, processing, and verifying all information. (For large directories, clerks were given responsibility for a specific alphabetical section of the book.) Not only did the new work arrangement improve the quality of the work experience of the employees, but the efficiency of the operation increased as well—in part because clerks made fewer errors and it was no longer necessary to have employees who merely checked and verified the work of others.

In recent years, work redesign increasingly is being used as one part of a larger change package aimed at improving the overall quality of worklife and productivity of people at work. A good case in point is the new General Foods pet food manufacturing plant in Topeka, Kansas. When plans were developed for the facility in the late 1960s, corporate management decided to design and manage the plant in full accord with state-of-the-art behavioral science knowledge. Non-traditional features were built into the plant from the beginning—involving the physical design of the facilities, the management style, information and feedback systems, compensation arrangements, and career paths for individual employees. A key part of the plan was the organization of the workforce into teams. Each team (consisting of seven to fourteen members) was given near-autonomous responsibility for a significant organizational task. In addition to actually carrying out the work required to complete the task, team members performed many activities that traditionally had been reserved for management—such as coping with manufacturing problems, distributing individual tasks among team members, screening and selecting new team members, participating in organizational decision-making, and so on.

The basic jobs to be performed by team members were designed to be as challenging as possible. Moreover, employees were encouraged to broaden their skills on a continuous basis so that they would become able to handle even more challenging work. While not without problems, the Topeka plant appears to be prospering—and many employees experience life in the organization as a pleasant and near-revolutionary change from their traditional ideas about what happens at work. (For more data on this example, see Chapter 12, "Case Histories.")

Work Redesign as a Strategy for Change

The redesign of work differs from most other behavioral science approaches to changing life in organizations in at least four ways. Together, these four points of uniqueness offer a rather compelling case for work redesign as a strategy for initiating organizational change.

1. *Work redesign alters the basic relationship between a person and what he or she does on the job:* When all the outer layers are stripped away, many organizational problems come to rest at the interface between people and the tasks they do. Frederick Taylor realized this when he set out to design and manage organizations "scientifically" at the beginning of the century. The design of work was central to the scientific management approach, and special pains were taken to ensure that workers' tasks did not exceed their performance capabilities. As the approach gained credence in the management community, new and sophisticated methodologies for analyzing work methods emerged, and industrial engineers forged numerous principles of work design. In general, these principles were intended to minimize the possibility of human error on the job (often by partitioning the work into small, simple segments), to minimize wasted time and motion, and thereby to maximize overall production efficiency.

It turned out, however, that workers often did not like jobs designed according to the dictates of scientific management. In effect, the person-job relationship had been arranged so that achieving the goals of the organization (i.e., high productivity) often meant sacrificing important personal goals (i.e., the opportunity for interesting, personally rewarding work). Taylor and his associates attempted to deal with this difficulty by installing financial incentive programs intended to make workers want to work hard toward organizational goals, and by placing such an elaborate set of supervisory controls on workers that they scarcely could behave otherwise. But the basic incongruence between the person and the work remained, and "people problems" (such as high absenteeism and turnover, poor quality work, high worker dissatisfaction) became increasingly evident in work organizations.

In the last several decades, industrial psychologists have carried out great quantities of research intended to overcome some of the problems that accompanied the spread of scientific management throughout the industrial sector of society. Sophisticated strategies for identifying those individuals most qualified to perform specific jobs have been developed and validated. New training and attitude change programs have been tried. And numerous motivational techniques have been proposed to increase the energy and commitment with which workers do their tasks—such as human relations programs, alteration of supervisory styles, and installation of complex piece rate and profit sharing incentive plans. None have proven fully successful. Indeed, as organizations have become larger (and as automated technologies have revolutionized the content of many jobs), some observers report that the quality of the work experience of employees today is more problematic than it was in the heyday of scientific management.

The redesign of work as a change strategy offers the opportunity to break out of the "givens" that have limited previous attempts to improve life at work. It is based on the assumption that the work itself may be one of the most profound influences on employee motivation, satisfaction and productivity. It acknowledges (and attempts to build upon) the fact that people are unable to set aside their social and emotional needs while at work. And it provides a strategy for moving away from extrinsic props to worker motivation—and instead toward internal work motivation, in which the worker does the work because it interests and challenges him, rewarding himself for a job well done when he performs effectively.

2. *Work redesign directly changes behavior—and it tends to stay changed:* People do the tasks they are given. How well they do them depends on many factors, including how the tasks themselves are designed. But people do them. On the other hand, people do not always behave consistently with their attitudes, their level of satisfaction, or what they cognitively "know" they

should do. Indeed, it is now well-established that one's attitudes often are determined by the behaviors one engages in—rather than vice-versa, as traditionally has been thought. This is especially the case when the individual perceives that he has substantial personal freedom or autonomy in choosing how he will behave.

Enriching jobs, then, may have a twin virtue. First, behavior itself is changed. And second, an increase usually is realized in the degree to which the individual experiences high levels of autonomy and personal discretion at work—increasing the likelihood that the individual will develop attitudes that are supportive of his new on-the-job behaviors.

The approach of work redesign does not rely on getting attitudes changed first (e.g., inducing the worker to "care more" about the work outcomes—as in zero defects programs) and hoping that the attitude change will generalize to work behavior. Instead, the strategy is to change the behavior itself, and to change it in a way that gradually leads to a more positive set of attitudes about the work, the organization, and the self.

Moreover, after jobs are changed, it usually is rather difficult for workers to slip back into old ways of proceeding. The old ways simply are inappropriate for the new tasks, and structure of those tasks reinforces the changes that have taken place. One need not worry much about the kind of backsliding that occurs so often after training or attitude modification activities, especially those that occur off-site. The stimuli that influence the worker's behavior are very much on-site, every hour of every day. And once those stimuli are changed, they are likely to stay that way—at least until the job is once again redesigned.

3. *Work redesign offers—indeed, often forces into one's hands—numerous opportunities for initiating other organizational changes:* When work is redesigned in an organization such that many people are doing things differently than they used to, new problems inevitably surface and demand attention. These can be constructed solely as problems—or they can be treated as opportunities for further organizational development activities. For example, technical problems are likely to develop when jobs are changed—of-

fering the opportunity to smooth and refine the work system as a system. Interpersonal issues are likely to arise, almost inevitably between supervisors and subordinates, but also between peers who now have to relate to one another in new ways. These offer the chance for developmental work aimed at improving the social and supervisory aspects of the work system.

Because such problems are literally forced to the surface by the job changes all parties may feel a need to do something about them. The "something" can range from using the existence of the problems as an occasion for declaring that "job enrichment doesn't work," to simply trying to solve the problems quickly so the project can proceed, to using the problems as a point of entry for attacking other organizational issues. If this last stance is taken, behavioral science professionals may find themselves pleasantly removed from the old difficulty of selling their wares to skeptical managers and employees who are not really sure there is anything wrong. And eventually a program of organizational change and development may evolve that addresses organizational systems and practices that superficially seem unrelated to how the work itself is designed.

4. *Work redesign, in the long term, can result in organizations that re-humanize rather than de-humanize the people who work in them:* Despite the popular over-blowing of the work ethic issue in recent years, the evidence is convincing that organizations can and do sometimes stamp out part of the humanness of their members— and especially that natural motivation toward growth and personal development that is so clearly present in infants. By the time children have finished school, or at least by the time they have done ten years in a work organization, their motivation toward personal growth and development may have been rendered near-latent.

Work redesign can help individuals regain the chance to experience the "kick" that comes from doing a job well, and can encourage them to once again care about their work and about developing the competence to do it even better. These payoffs from work redesign go well beyond simple "job satisfaction." Cows grazing in the field may be satisfied, and employees in organizations can be made just as satisfied by paying them well, by keeping bosses off their backs, by putting them in pleasant work rooms with pleasant people, and by arranging things so that the days pass without undue stress or strain.

The kind of satisfaction at issue here is different. It is a satisfaction that develops only when an individual is stretching and growing as a human being, increasing his sense of his own competence and self-worth. Whether creation of opportunities for personal growth is legitimate as a goal for work redesign activities is a value question deserving long discussion; the case for the vaue of work redesign strictly in terms of organizational health easily can rest on the first three points discussed above. But personal growth is without question a central component of the overall quality of worklife in organizations, and the impact of work design on the people who do the work—as human beings—should be neither overlooked nor underemphasized.

In Perspective

Two documents well worth reading in this area are *The Worker and the Job: Coping with Change*[1] and *Work in America*,[2] a 1972 special task force report to the Secretary of Health, Education and Welfare.

The latter states:

> The redesign of jobs is the keystone of this report. Not only does it hold out some promise to decrease mental and physical health costs, increase productivity, and improve the quality of life for millions of Americans at all occupational levels (but also) it would give, for the first time, a voice to many workers in an important decision-making process.

Redesign of jobs usually involves reorganizing work along the following lines:

> Offering the individual worker more voice and responsibility in decision making that pertains to his job;
>
> Making the job itself more challenging and more of a whole set of interconnected tasks or a whole segment of work rather than a fragment;
>
> Setting up small work groups to increase the individual's

sense of belonging and permit working as a team member responsible for a significant, identifiable output;

Breaking down the traditional status barriers between management and production or support personnel;

Promoting from within whenever feasible to recognize, encourage and reward persons capable of advancement.

DOES WORK REDESIGN WORK?

Unfortunately, existing research literature and case reports on the topic are not very helpful in assessing the validity of the claims made by either the advocates or the skeptics of work redesign. In particular, examination of the literature leads to the following conclusions:

Reports of work redesign successes tend to be more evangelical than thoughtful: little conceptualizing is done that would be useful either as a guide to implementation of work redesign or as a conceptual base for research on its effects.

The methodologies used in evaluating organizational changes using work redesign often are weak or incomplete. Therefore, findings reported usually are ambiguous to some degree and open to numerous alternative explanations.

Although informal sources and surveys suggest that the failure rate for work redesign projects is moderate to high, few documented analyses of projects that failed are available. This is particularly unfortunate because careful analyses of failures often are among the most effective ways to learn about the applicability and the consequences of organizational change strategies.

Most published reports focus almost exclusively on assessing the positive and negative effects of certain changes in work content. Conclusions are then drawn about the general worth of work redesign as a change strategy. Yet is is inevitable that the way such changes are installed and the nature of the broader organizational setting interact with the content of the changes in determining their ultimate impact. Existing literature has little to say about the nature or dynamics of that interaction.

Rarely are economic data (i.e., direct and indirect dollar costs and benefits) analyzed and discussed when conclusions are drawn about the effects of work redesign projects—even though many such projects originally are undertaken because of anticipated economic gains.

In sum, it appears that despite the abundance of writing on the topic, little is known for sure about why work redesign is effective when it is, what goes wrong when it isn't, and how the strategy can be altered to improve its general usefulness as an approach to personal and organizational change.

HOW WORK REDESIGN CAN IMPROVE SATISFACTION, MOTIVATION, AND PRODUCTIVITY

Because work redesign potentially can contribute to the improvement of worklife and productivity in a number of different ways, the particular type of theory that will be most useful in a given instance will depend substantially on the type of problem addressed and the kind of change contemplated. There are three different avenues for achieving personal and organizational change through the redesign of work.

The first avenue focuses on how work redesign can minimize the negative consequences of work that is highly routine and repetitive. The second examines ways that work can be changed to provide new or increased opportunities for positive and self-sustaining work motivation and productivity. The third avenue deals with ways that the social and technical aspects of the workplace can be changed in concert, to simultaneously enrich both the content and the context of the work. Thus, the first avenue attempts to eliminate actively negative outcomes of work; the second attempts to create new and positive outcomes; and the third takes a step back from the individual job and attempts to develop healthier work systems.

Minimizing the Effects of Repetitive Work

Highly repetitive jobs have been found to diminish worker alertness, to decrease sensitivity to sensory input, and in some cases to impair muscular coordination. Because employees dislike work on such jobs, they often engage in behaviors aimed at countering their feeling of boredom—such as daydreaming, chatting with other workers, making frequent readjustments of posture and position, finding excuses to take unnecessary breaks from work, and so on. Many such behaviors impair the work effectiveness of the employee—and, at that, result in only temporary relief from the boredom of the job.

Psychologists have amassed a great deal of research evidence about the antecedents and consequences of heightened and depressed levels of psychological and physiological activation. Such findings are helpful in understanding the reasons for the frequently dysfunctional effects of repetitive jobs. Moreover, it may be possible to draw on activation theory to plan alterations in the stimulus characteristics of jobs such that an individual experiences a near-optimal level of activation in his work (i.e., neither boredom nor excessive stimulation).

Yet despite the clear relevance of activation theory to job design, three thorny problems must be overcome before the theory can be applied to real-world jobs. The first problem has to do with differences among individuals in how activated they are by their jobs, and in the level of activation they find preferable. The research literature shows clearly that different people have different "optimal levels" of activation (that is, the level at which a person is most alert, neither bored nor over-stimulated). Moreover, there is increasing evidence that a person's personality affects how he will act when he is over- or under-stimulated. Such differences among people are obviously important in applying activation theory to job redesign, yet at the moment the theory provides little explicit guidance about how individual differences should be dealt with in designing jobs and tasks.

Secondly, means must be developed for measuring current levels of activation of individuals in work settings. Although some progress on this issue has been made, it remains very difficult to reliably measure how near an individual is to his optimal level of activation. And until better measurement techniques are developed, it will remain impractical to use the theory as a basis for the redesign of jobs except in a very gross fashion—e.g., in instances where it is clear that most employees are enormously over- or under-stimulated by their work.

Finally, some practical difficulties in applying the theory are encountered because of the processes by which individuals adapt to changes in the level of stimulation they experience. A person's level of activation decreases markedly as a function of familiarity with a given stimulus situation—but after a period of rest, re-presentation of the same stimulus situation will once again raise the level of activation. More complete understanding of the waxing and waning of activation in various circumstances could have many implications for job design practices—for example, the practice of job rotation. Those who advocate job rotation claim that work motivation can be kept reasonably high by rotating individuals through several different jobs, even though each of the jobs would become monotonous and boring if one were to remain on it for a long period of time. If future research can identify ways to maintain activation at near-optimal levels through planned stimulus change, then the theory can contribute substantially to increasing the usefulness on job rotation as a motivational technique. If, however, it turns out that there are general and inevitable decreases in activation over time regardless of how different tasks and rest periods are cycled, then the long-term usefulness of the technique would seem limited.

Creating Conditions for Positive Work Motivation and Personal Growth

Even if the problems with activation theory identified above are solved, the theory still would appear useful mainly for alleviating negative outcomes that result from under- or over-stimulating jobs. The theory offers little guidance toward the design of work that will elicit positive and self-reinforcing work motivation. Two conceptual approaches to work redesign that do attempt to specify the conditions under which positive work motivation can be generated and maintained are reviewed below, namely, motivation-hygiene theory and job characteristics theory.

Motivation-hygiene theory: By far the most influential theory of work redesign has been the Herzberg two-factor theory of satisfaction and motivation. In essence, the theory proposes that the primary determinants of employee satisfaction are factors intrinsic to the work that is done—i.e., recognition, achievement, responsibility, advancement, personal growth in competence. These factors are called "motivators" because employees are motivated to obtain more of them—for example, through good job performance. Dissatisfaction, on the other hand, is seen as being caused by "hygiene factors" that are extrinsic to the work itself. Examples include company policies, supervisory practices, pay plans, working conditions, and so on. The Herzberg theory specifies that a job will enhance work motivation only to the degree that "motivators" are designed into the work itself. Changes that deal solely with "hygiene" factors should not generate increases in employee motivation.

It is much to the credit of the Herzberg theory that it has prompted a great deal of research, and inspired a number of successful change projects involving the redesign of work. Especially noteworthy is the series of job enrichment studies done at AT&T. These studies provide demonstration, for a diversity of jobs, that job enrichment can lead to benefical outcomes both for the individuals involved and for the organization itself. Moreover, a set of step-by-step procedures for implementing job enrichment were generated as part of the AT&T program, and these procedures continue to guide many work redesign activities throughout the country.

The Herzberg theory (specifically the distinction between motivators and hygiene factors) provides a clear and straightforward way of thinking about employee motivation, and for predicting the likely impact of various planned changes on motivation. The phrases "Yes, but that's really only a hygiene factor. . . ." and "But would it change the work itself?" have undoubtedly been used thousands of times as managers consider various strategies for attempting to improve employee work motivation. More often than not, applying the Herzberg theory has helped keep change focused on issues that are central rather than peripheral to work motivation.

A case in point is the analysis of such recently popular innovations as the four-day work week and flexible scheduling of working hours. Both of these changes legitimately can be viewed as devices intended to improve the quality of the overall work experience of employees in organizations. They provide workers with increased flexibility in planning leisure activities, in coordinating work and family responsibilities, and generally in achieving a higher level of personal control over one's life. As is the case for most significant organizational innovations, early reports of the effects of the four-day week and flexible work scheduling have been optimistic.

Yet the Herzberg theory would suggest that such alterations of work schedules are not likely to lead to long-term improvements in worker satisfaction, motivation, or productivity. The reason is that the nature of the work itself is not changed by such innovations. And if the work itself is more frustrating than fulfilling, then about all that could be expected from flexible scheduling of work hours would be: (a) a decrease in dissatisfaction resulting from person/work conflicts (which of course is an item of great consequence to many individuals) and (b) the opportunity to schedule in breaks from work, so that any dysfunctional consequences arising from the repetitive nature of the work could be attenuated. Similarly, a four-day week might be expected to decrease some dissatisfactions arising from person/work conflicts—but also would not help with problems that derive from dissatisfying aspects of the work itself. Indeed, because each work day would be longer under a four-day arrangement, such problems might be exacerbated rather than relieved. After the novelty of the four-day week had worn off, the net result might only be a change from "TGIF" to "Thank God it's Thursday."

What the Herzberg theory does, and does well, is point attention directly to the enormous significance of the work itself as a factor in the ultimate motivation and satisfaction of employees. And because the message of the theory is simple, persuasive, and directly relevant to the design and evaluation of actual organizational changes, the theory continues to be widely-known and generally used by managers of organizations in this country.

Yet despite its considerable merit, there are a number of difficulties with the motivation-hygiene theory that compromise its usefulness. For one, a number of researchers have been unable to provide empirical support for the major tenets of the two-factor theory itself.

In particular, it appears that the original dichotomization of aspects of the workplace into "motivators" and "hygiene factors" may have been partly due to methodological artifact. Moreover, some aspects of the workplace can at times serve as motivators, and at other times as hygiene factors. Non-specific praise from a supervisor, or an end-of-year raise in pay, for example, would not be classified as motivators by the theory. Yet to the extent that praise or pay raises are provided by the organization (and experienced by the employee) as recognition for achievement, such items would help motivate the employee—because "recognition" is included in the theory as a motivator. Thus, the motivating factors are not operationally defined in and of themselves; instead, the status of various factors depends in large part on the dynamics of the particular organizational situation.

This difficulty severely compromises the degree to which the presence or absence of the motivating factors can be measured for existing jobs. At the least, the measurement problem makes empirical test of the theory in organizations very difficult. It also raises severe practical difficulties in using the theory to plan and implement actual job changes—because there is no way systematically to diagnose the status of jobs prior to change, or to measure the effects of job enrichment activities on the jobs themselves after the change has been carried out.

Finally, the theory does not provide for differences among people in how responsive they are likely to be to enriched jobs. In the AT&T studies based on the theory, for example, it was assumed that the motivating factors potentially could increase the work motivation of all employees—although the implementation procedures devised for these studies specified that enriching tasks should be added to a job only when the employee showed "readiness" for the new responsibilities. But the theory itself has not yet been elaborated to specify how such determinations of readiness should be made. Because evidence is now abundant that some individuals are more likely to respond positively to an enriched, complex job than are others, it would seem imperative that the theory be elaborated to specify in concrete terms how phenomena of individual differences should be dealt with—both conceptually, and in the design and implementation of actual changes.

Job characteristics theory: An approach to work redesign that focuses on the objective characteristics of jobs is rooted in the work of Turner and Lawrence. These researchers developed objective measures of a number of job characteristics that were predicted to relate positively to employee satisfaction and attendance. The job characteristics were summarized in a single measure (called the RTA Index) that reflects the overall complexity and challenge of the work.

Expected positive relationships between the RTA Index and employee satisfaction and attendance were found only for workers from factories located in small towns. For employees in urban work settings, satisfaction was inversely related to the scores of jobs on the RTA Index, and absenteeism was unrelated to the Index. The investigators concluded that reactions to "good" (i.e., high RTA Index) jobs were moderated by differences in the subcultural backgrounds of employees.

A study by Hackman and Lawler[3] provided further evidence that job characteristics can directly affect employee attitudes and behavior at work, and suggested that such effects could be conceptualized in terms of the expectancy theory of motivation. Specifically, they predicted that if certain "core" job characteristics are present, employees will experience a positive, self-generated affective response when they perform well—and that this internal "kick" will provide an incentive for continued efforts toward good performance. The specific job dimensions proposed as necessary to create conditions for such self-motivation to develop and be maintained are: (a) variety, (b) task identity (i.e., doing a whole piece of work), (c) autonomy, and (d) feedback.

In addition, Hackman and Lawler suggested that obtained differences in how various sub-cultural groups of employees react to complex jobs might be most simply explained by how strongly group members desired personal growth and development. It was predicted that the stronger an employee's need for growth, the more he would value the feeling of personal accomplishment obtained from doing his job well—and therefore the more likely he would be to respond positively to a job high on the four core dimensions.

Results for employees in a telephone company generally supported the prediction that employees who work on jobs high on the core dimensions exhibit high work motivation, satisfaction, performance, and attendance. In addition, Hackman and Lawler found that a number of dependent measures were moderated as predicted by growth need strength: that is, employees with high measured needs for growth responded more positively to "good" jobs than did employees low in growth need strength.

A model of work design that attempts to extend, refine and systematize the findings described above has been proposed by Hackman and Oldham. In essence, the model proposes that five core job characteristics (skill variety, task identity, task significance, autonomy, feedback) foster certain work experiences for the employee which, in turn, affect his work motivation and satisfaction. Job redesign activities based on the model involve increasing the standing of a job on the core job characteristics, especially for employees who have strong growth needs.

The job characteristics model (like the Herzberg approach) deals only with aspects of jobs that can be altered to create positive motivational incentives for the job incumbent. It does not directly address the dysfunctional aspects of repetitive work (as does activation theory), although presumably a job designed in accord with the dictates of the model would not turn out to be excessively routine or repetitive.

In addition, both the motivation-hygiene and the job characteristics models focus exclusively on the relationship between an individual and his work. These theories do not explicitly address managerial, social, technical, or situational moderators of how people react to their work—even though attention to such factors would be critical to the successful installation of work redesign programs in on-going organizations.

Finally, both the Herzberg and the job characteristics models are framed in such a way as to apply exclusively to jobs that are done more-or-less independently by individuals. They offer no guidelines for the effective design of work for interacting teams—such as when the work involves interdependent contributions from a number of employees, and the job is more appropriately conceived of as a group task than as an individual task.

NOTES

1. *The Worker and the Job: Coping With Change,* The 1973 American Assembly Background Papers (Prentice-Hall, 1974).

2. *Work in America* (Cambridge, MA: The MIT Press, 1972).

3. Hackman, J. R. and Lawler, E. E., "Employee Reactions to Job Characteristics," *Journal of Applied Psychology Monograph,* 55 (1971) 259-286.

Guidelines for Introducing
Work Redesign

The material in this chapter is based on "Improving the Quality of Worklife . . . and in the Process, Improving Productivity," prepared for the Manpower Administration, U.S. Department of Labor, by Edward M. Glaser, Human Interaction Institute, and published as PB 236 209, August, 1974.

A number of experts—on job enrichment and improving the quality of worklife—have suggested guidelines for introducing such programs. Five of these guidelines will be summarized here.

While there are differences in philosophy, emphasis and strategies, the area of agreement is considerably greater than that of disagreement. Two of the interesting disagreements are: (1) University of Utah Professor Frederick Herzberg (until 1972 at Case Western Reserve), argues against inviting direct participation by the employees whose jobs are to be enriched, while most other students and practitioners in the field favor it; (2) Neal Herrick, formerly of the Department of Labor, now at Ohio State University, argues strongly for employees to share in cost-savings; a number of others do not consider this essential. The fifth set of guidelines presented here attempts to integrate what has been learned, as well as present some special emphases.

LOUIS E. DAVIS GUIDELINES

Professor Davis[1] of UCLA's Graduate School of Management reviewed six studies "intended to indicate the multidimensionality of the job design problem and the pervasiveness of its influence on quantity and quality of output, costs, and job satisfaction." He concluded that performance improves:

1. When job and organization designs lead to responsible autonomous job behavior. Responsible behavior as defined here implies acceptance of responsibility by the individual for the cycle of activities required to complete the product or service. Autonomous behavior encompasses self-regulation of work content and structure within the job where the job is an assignment having inputs, facilities and outputs; self-evaluation of performance; self-adjustment to changes required by technological variability; participation in setting up of goals or objectives for job outputs.

2. When there is acceptance of responsibility for rate, quantity or quality of output.

3. When there is recognition of interdependence of the individual or group on others for effective progress of the cycle of activity.

4. When the scope of jobs includes all tasks required to complete a part, product or service.

5. When the job content includes all four types of tasks inherent in productive work: (a) auxiliary or service (supply, tooling), (b) preparatory (setup), (c) processing or transformation, and (d) control (inspection).

6. When the tasks included in the job content permit closure of the activity, if not product completion, permitting development of identity with product or process.

7. When there is the introduction of task variety in the form of larger numbers and kinds of tasks and skills as well as more complex tasks.

8. When product quality acceptance is within the authority of the jobholder.

9. When there is social interaction among job holders and communication with peers and supervisors.

10. When there is a reward system that supports responsible autonomy.

In addition to the above items which relate to job structure, the following aspects of organizational design were cited as contributing to improved performance:

1. Group composition that permits self-regulation of the group functioning.

2. Group composition that deliberately provides for the full range of skills required to carry out all the tasks in an activity cycle.

3. Delegation of authority (formal and informal) to the group for self-assignment of tasks and roles to group members.

4. Group structure that permits internal communication.

5. A group reward system for joint output.

The conditions summarized by Dr. Davis call for the proper climate within an organization; a climate in which top management supports wholeheartedly the development and implementation of those conditions.

A general caution: In any quality of work program management cannot delegate its responsibility for successful operation when it gives workers autonomy and the power to regulate and evaluate themselves. To carry out this responsibility properly, top management needs an information system to provide facts on such items as a scrap, rework or reject rate, sales trends, expenses, inventories, profits and whatever else may be necessary for intelligent and timely monitoring. In this way, inquiry and new problem-solving action can be devised if called for.

FREDERICK HERZBERG GUIDELINES

University of Utah psychologist Frederick Herzberg[2] suggests the following steps:

1. Select those jobs in which (a) the investment in industrial engineering does not make changes too costly, (b) attitudes are poor, (c) hygiene is becoming very costly, and (d) motivation will make a difference in performance.

2. Approach these jobs with conviction that they can be changed. Years of tradition have led management to believe that the content of the jobs is sacrosanct and the only scope of action that they have is in ways of stimulating people.

3. Brainstorm a list of changes that may enrich the job without concern for their practicality.

4. Screen the list to eliminate suggestions that involve "hy-

giene" rather than actual motivation. ("Hygiene" refers to job surroundings or "maintenance" or *context*, depicted by the line of the chart which follows; motivation refers to the job *content*—the lower line on the chart on page 80.)

5. Screen the list for generalities, such as "give them more responsibility," that are rarely followed in practice. . . .

6. Screen the list to eliminate any horizontal loading suggestions.

7. Avoid direct participation by the employees whose jobs are to be enriched. Ideas they have expressed previously certainly constitute a valuable source for recommended changes, but their direct involvement contaminates the process with human relations *hygiene* and more specifically gives them only a *sense* of making a contribution. Their job is to be changed and it is the content that will produce the motivation, not attitudes about being involved or challenged inherent in setting up the job. That process will be over shortly and it is what the employees will be doing from then on that will determine their motivation. A sense of participation will result only in short-term movement.

8. In the initial attempts at job enrichment, set up a controlled experiment. At least two equivalent groups should be chosen: one an experimental unit in which the motivators are systematically introduced over a period of time, and the other one a control group in which no changes are made. For both groups hygiene should be allowed to follow its natural course for the duration of the experiment. Pre- and post-installation tests of performance and job attitudes are needed to evaluate the effectiveness of the job enrichment program.

9. Be prepared for a drop in performance in the experimental group in the first few weeks. The changeover to a new job may lead to a temporary reduction in efficiency.

10. Expect your first-line supervisors to experience some anxiety and hostility over the changes you are making. . . . After a successful experiment, however, the supervisor usually discovers the supervisory and managerial functions he has neglected or which were never his because all his time was given over to checking the work of his subordinates. . . .

Guide for Determining Motivation and Maintenance Items

1. Perceived fairness of pay
2. Working conditions
3. Administrative practices
4. Job security
5. Fringe benefits
6. Satisfaction/dissatisfaction with interpersonal relations
7. Status factors
8. Character of supervision

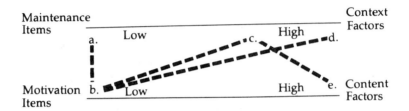

1. Sense of achievement
2. Recognition for achievement
3. Opportunities for advancement
4. Opportunities for increased responsibility
5. Satisfaction with the work itself
6. Feeling of continued learning and growth

Herzberg's theory of motivation-hygiene factors can be diagramed by starting with two parallel lines as above. The top line represents the hygiene or maintenance or context factors surrounding the job. The bottom line represents the motivation or content factors inherent in the work itself.

If both are low, as in a.---b., then productivity, morale and quality of output are likely to be low.

If an organization offers outstanding advantages in the maintenance items but does nothing to upgrade the motivation items (b.---d.), dissatisfactions are likely to be reduced, at least temporarily, but intrinsic satisfactions with the work will not be improved, with a likely result of raising costs appreciably but not gaining a commensurate increase in productivity or any sustained improvement in morale.

If an organization can arrange its modus operandi in a way that optimizes or significantly enhances the motivation or content items, and also sees to it that the maintenance or context items are well above average, as in c.---e., then productivity and morale are likely to rise in a sustained way. The work force not only will have dissatisfactions removed or reduced, but even more important, they will have a rich fare of intrinsic motivators.

ELI GINZBERG OBSERVATIONS

Eli Ginzberg[3], professor of economics at Columbia University, and four Ford Foundation staff members traveled through the Netherlands, Sweden, Norway, France, Italy and Israel in 1972 to observe some of the work restructuring experiments in these countries.

Ginzberg writes:

> As for the workers, why have they been willing to participate in experiments that could not be launched and surely could not be successfully implemented without their cooperation? What have they seen as their own possible gain in all this? To begin with, most factory work in Europe—as in the U.S.—leaves much to be desired. It is characterized by excessive noise, poor ventilation, frequent breakdowns in machinery, poor supervision, infrequent rest periods, and a host of other conditions workers finds irksome. As a result, any effort on the part of management to address itself to these problems, provided the workers are convinced that the new approach is not aimed at getting them to produce more without commensurate adjustment in wages, will be seen as a boon. The fact that most experiments require the cooperation of only small numbers of workers— those who volunteer for them—makes it considerably easier to convince them on this point.
>
> The volunteers frequently respond to improved communications and expanded decision-making powers, which are an integral part of many work structuring experiments. They like the idea of having more say about the specifics of the production process: and they enjoy the regularly scheduled conferences at which they learn

about how their work fits into the larger picture. They also like the fact that the experiments relieve them of one or more layers of supervision and that they're given more room for initiative. In the case of autonomous work groups—a leading form of experimentation—the members frequently enjoy the camaraderie that develops, and most of them find themselves under less pressure than before, when the pace of work was set by the machine.

Four important principles noted by Ginzberg and others are: (1) the workers—and the unions, in organized situations—need to be convinced that the new approach is not aimed at getting them to produce more just to benefit management, (2) participation in quality of work improvement should be voluntary, for those who wish to have more voice and take more responsibility in the company, (3) the focus of work-structuring experiments should be improvement of conditions which the workers have participated in identifying as unsatisfactory, (4) one clear result should be the opportunity for more initiative and more voice in job-related decisions by the work force.

HERRICK AND MACCOBY SUGGESTIONS

Neal Herrick and Dr. Michael Maccoby[4] of Harvard listed four principles which they believe underlie the humanization of work:

1. *Security:* The worker's freedom from anxiety concerning his health, safety, income and future employment.

2. *Equity:* The employee receives compensation commensurate to his contribution to the value of service or product.

3. *Individuation:* Work should stimulate the development of the individual's unique abilities and capacity for craftsmanship rather than force him into a mechanized role. It should include continued learning rather than boredom and stagnation. The principle of individuation, once adopted, can lead to a non-bureaucratic spirit in which workers are encouraged to develop themselves and to learn as much as they wish about the industry as a whole. . . . The desire for craftsmanship is one of the deep strengths of the American character.

By weakening it, we have lessened ourselves as a people. Recent studies of worker attitudes have clearly shown worker's concern that their jobs be more interesting, provide more autonomy and allow them to develop their abilities. After a certain level of income is reached, these concerns are more important than receiving money.

4. *Democracy:* The principle of democracy, like that of individuation, is opposed to making the worker into a passive object, a machine part. It implies psychological activeness. Wherever technically possible, workers should manage themselves. Authoritarian, hierarchical control should be replaced by cooperative self-managed groups. Autonomous work groups should replace pyramidal structures. Where supervisors are necessary, they should be elected directly by the workers.

Herrick and Maccoby contended that a system based on these four principles "would develop in the worker a sense of hope, activeness, and productiveness."

RICHARD E. WALTON NOTATIONS

Harvard University professor Richard E. Walton, who also has served as consultant to many industrial firms and government agencies in the field of applied behavioral science, offers the following summary:[5]

> . . .Employees increasingly want their work to be characterized by challenge, mutual influence patterns, dignity, positive social relevance, balanced attention to emotionality and rationality, and cooperative social patterns. In order to substantially increase these ingredients, the work situation must undergo comprehensive change. Piecemeal reforms, such as job enrichment, management by objectives, and sensitivity training are inadequate.
>
> The organization redesign should be systemic. First, redesign must focus on the division of labor, involving, for example, the formation of self-managing work teams, re-creation of whole tasks by reversing the trend toward

fractionation of work, and an increase in the flexibility in work assignments by a variety of means.

Second, the redesign must embrace supporting elements, such as a trimming of supervision and more delegation of authority. Also, the information and reward schemes must be tailored to facilitate the delegation of decision making and to reinforce team work.

Third, other elements in the work situation must enhance the status of workers and communicate trust in their exercise of self-control—e.g., salaried payroll and no time clock. Similarly, recruitment and/or training are required to ensure the necessary skills.

Obviously, the revisions in these many elements must be coordinated and must result in a new, internally consistent whole.

The impetus for work restructuring experiments of this kind comes from prior philosophical commitment, an interest in the behavioral sciences, and compelling personnel or productivity problems.

A number of conditions are favorable to the introduction of such experiments: new plants with small, nonunionized work forces, located in rural communities geographically separate from other parts of the firm. None of these are necessary conditions, but each facilitates the rapid introduction of the innovative work system.

By design of the sample, the experiments reviewed in this study reportedly produced positive results in the first year or two of their existence—in terms of both quality of worklife and productivity indexes.

However, several of the experimental units suffered setbacks after an initially successful introduction. A number of factors can threaten termination or create regression in these innovations: a lack of internal consistency in the original design; loss of hierarchical support; loss in internal leadership and skills; heightened stress and crisis; tensions with various parties external to the unit; an unfavorable ratio of psychological costs to benefits for individual participants; and isolation resulting from a failure to diffuse. With foreplanning, sponsors and leaders of innovative work can minimize the potential threats listed above.

J. RICHARD HACKMAN, GREG OLDHAM, ROBERT JANSON AND KENNETH PURDY'S "A NEW STRATEGY FOR JOB ENRICHMENT"[6]

This is a report of a three-year study, funded jointly by the U.S. Department of Labor and the Office of Naval Research, on a new strategy for going about the redesign of production and clerical work.

The researchers posit three "psychological states" as critical in determining a person's motivation and satisfaction on the job. They are:

1. *Experienced meaningfulness:* The individual must perceive his work as worthwhile or important by some system of values he accepts.
2. *Experienced responsibility:* He must believe that he personally is accountable for the outcome of his efforts.
3. *Knowledge of results:* He must be able to determine, on some fairly regular basis, whether or not the outcome of his work activities are satisfactory.

When all three of these conditions are high, then internal work motivation, job satisfaction and work quality all tend to be high, while absenteeism and turnover are low. When one or more of these three psychological states are low, motivation drops markedly.

The authors identify five core job dimensions that contribute to a job's meaningfulness for the worker. They are: (1) Skill Variety (the degree to which a job requires the worker to perform activities which challenge his skills and abilities); (2) Task Identity (the degree to which the job requires completion of a "whole" and identifiable piece of work); (3) Task Significance (the degree to which the job has a substantial and perceivable impact on the lives of other people); (4) Increased Personal Responsibility (the degree to which the job gives the worker freedom, independence and discretion in scheduling work and determining how he will carry it out); (5) Feedback (the degree to which a worker, in carrying out the work activities required by the job, gets information about the effectiveness of his efforts).

Hackman and Oldham have developed a package of diagnostic instruments called the "Job Diagnostic Survey (JDS)" which includes a test to measure Motivating Potential. This test provides a single summary index (MPS) of the degree to which the objective characteristics of the job will prompt high internal work motivation. However, "not everyone is able to become internally motivated in his work, even when the Motivating Potential of a job is very high indeed. . . . But . . . we believe that the organization . . . should provide the individual with the chance to reverse that trend whenever it can."

The JDS also provides a score on each of the five Core Dimensions described above.

In addition to the MPS score and the Core Dimensions score, the JDS provides measures of how people feel about other aspects of the work setting, such as pay, supervision and relations with coworkers. Finally, a score is provided to indicate the level of growth need strength of the employees. As Hackman and Oldham have noted, "Employees who have strong growth needs are more likely to be more responsive to job enrichment than employees with weak growth needs. Therefore, it is important to know at the outset just what kinds of satisfactions the people who do the job are (and are not) motivated to obtain from their work. This will make it possible to identify which persons are best to start changes with, and which may need help in adapting to the new enriched job."

To translate the diagnostic information which can be gathered from the JDS, the authors suggest five "Implementing Concepts" for job enrichment. Each one is a specific action step aimed at improving both the quality of the working experience for the individual and his work productivity. They are:

1. Forming natural work units; autonomy.

2. Combining tasks (for individuals or small *teams*); task identity.

3. Establishing direct relationships with the "clients" or ultimate users of the work group's product or service; task significance.

4. Vertical loading, through which as many as practicable of the responsibilities and controls which formerly were reserved for higher levels of management are added to the job; skill variety.

5. Opening feedback channels, by means of which individual task teams can learn directly whether their performance is improving, deteriorating or remaining at a constant level; feedback from the job itself.

The authors report favorable findings on the questions of whether their job enrichment theory is correct (that is, seems to work out in practice), and whether their suggested change strategy really leads to measurable differences when it is applied in actual organizational settings.

INTEGRATION AND RECOMMENDATIONS—EDWARD GLASER AND ASSOCIATES

The efforts of Edward Glaser and Associates[7] toward promoting the quality of worklife and productivity improvement have focused on the following goals:

(1) Trying to elicit the understanding, commitment and support of the concept at the highest management level but *at least* at the highest level in the division, department or plant where a quality of worklife improvement program or job enrichment program is to be tried; (2) serving as a resource and catalyst in arranging for a company interested in exploring a job enrichment or worklife improvement effort to visit some other companies that have worked out successful, sustained programs of this type, and recommending some relevant reading, such as the Hackman and Oldham report, *Work in America, The Worker and the Job*, and this report with its case descriptions; (3) working with management to develop practicable ways of inviting the members of any given work group to

participate in problem identification, problem solving, goal setting and appropriate decision making—and in unionized situations, helping to develop a modus operandi that is likely to elicit union support and participation; (4) structuring the work where practicable and desirable into relatively small, 5-25 person task-group teams *if that evolves from step three;* (5) providing open channels for communication and systematic feedback of progress to all concerned; (6) offering the special resources of a knowledgeable and experienced consultant to the task teams wherever wanted or needed; (7) serving as a resource to the organization for their consideration of incentives, perhaps through a share in rewards derived from any *resultant* cost savings, increased productivity, or profits; (8) helping all concerned to keep an "eye on the ball," the ball being to enhance the organization's effectiveness and efficiency in task performance as well as to manifest creative concern for the quality of working life and the quality of contribution to societal well-being. Also, helping all constituencies perceive ways in which they can "win" simultaneously: customers, company, work group, individuals, unions if the work site is unionized, investors, and public—without the gains to any one group being at the expense of others.

From our experiences—and a review of the experiences of others—we draw the following observations, which can constitute guidelines for introducing a job redesign or quality of work improvement program:

1. If long-term gains are to be made and maintained, the top manager of the company, or of whatever division, department or subsidiary may be interested in a quality of work program, needs to understand and give sustained commitment to the philosophy and practice of that program.

2. Once the high-level decision is made to explore ways of operating under a philosophy of invited employee participation in job design, work structure, or whatever aspects of the operation seem appropriate, then all concerned, from the top down, need to understand the concept and become colleagues in planning the implementation program. Detailed preparation, planning, supervisory training and follow-up— all of which take time—are needed to achieve real improvement in quality of worklife criteria, work practices, job con-

tent and, in some cases, the organizational setup. In a company where the work force are union members, a sincere effort should be made to invite the union's collaboration.

An easy and natural way to start all this is for the top person in a given work group to invite the personnel within his jurisdiction to meet in an unhurried, freewheeling atmosphere to take stock, identify problems, evaluate performance, recommend solutions to problems, set goals, and think broadly about how to improve the quality of worklife while at the same time improving the effectiveness and efficiency of the organization. Subsequent meetings can carry this procedure down through the organization. The main purpose of the program should be to encourage/involve the members of task groups to become ego-involved or a participant in helping to improve the quality of their worklife. Then, at the same time, to improve the effectiveness, efficiency and productivity of the organization so that it can survive, be in a good position to share its success with the work force, better serve its customers and society. The attitudinal component of this is nondefensive encouragement and reinforcement for constructive challenge of standard procedures in a continual quest for improvement and excellence in any aspect of organizational or operational performance.

A company's readiness to embark on any worklife improvement program must be carefully assessed before deciding what steps may be appropriate to initiate. In some situations, a survey of employee perceptions and their suggestions for improvement, along with the setting up of some program for constructive follow-through, would be a simple way to invite broader employee participation. At other companies there may be readiness to try more comprehensive experiments in job enrichment—such as forming natural work units, combining tasks, planning and controlling the work to a large extent rather than just "doing" it. In still other situations it may be desirable to invite employees to review standard practices, such as work rules, discipline specifications, fringe benefit arrangements, etc.

A survey, if undertaken, could be part of an overall organizational development effort. It might include a small Task Force or Commission, often best set up with membership from various levels, to: (a) review (become familiar with) objectives, plans and programs of the organization or segment of the organization being studied; (b) interview administrators and staff at all levels to identify problems, perceptions of probable causes, and recommendations for improvement; (c) supplement personal interviews with a carefully constructed, brief questionnaire to a broader sample—or to anyone in the organization who wishes to respond; (d) feedback the findings in coherent form to management and then to whoever else might appropriately be involved; (e) implement "breakthrough" projects or pilot efforts or new policies/procedures to meet important identified problems—again involving interested persons from various levels; (f) monitor, ascertain, evaluate and feed back results from any changes made; (g) repeat the process of organizational assessment from time to time in a never-ending pursuit of development, improvement and renewal.

3. One of the best ways to begin for a company interested in pursuing quality of worklife improvement through work restructuring is by having some personal contact and interaction with respected kindred organizations which have successful "living demonstrations" of such programs. A special study team of interested personnel (rather than any single individual) should be invited to volunteer to *visit other such companies.* Background reading, such as: *The Failure of Success* edited by Alfred Marrow, AMACOM, New York, 1972; the HEW 1972 task force report on *Work in America;* and Robert Ford's *Motivation Through the Work Itself,* American Management Association, 1969; The American Assembly's *The Worker and the Job,* 1974; Hackman and Oldham's *A New Strategy for Job Enrichment,* 1974; then will be more meaningful.

4. The entire task group with which a quality of worklife program is to be implemented, not just the volunteer study team, should be invited to develop criteria for effective group performance. They also should have a voice in establishing ways to get baseline evaluation of existing performance, and ways to measure periodic progress. Consultants who are skillful in group process, problem solving, the introduction of change and evaluation—whether they are internal or external to the organization—can be helpful here.

5. The greatest productivity gains over time often have come through product design and methods improvement. Such improvements are likely to be boosted appreciably when the work force members (not just the engineers) are invited to participate in those efforts. Therefore, the newly created task groups should receive training in product design, methods improvement, quality standards, and effective ways of meeting those standards for whatever they are doing, as well as training in problem solving, listening skills and conflict resolution. They also should receive frequent feedback. How does their performance measure up to the agreed-upon criteria in comparison with baseline data? This should be coupled with praise/recognition/reward/positive reinforcement for any gains made—even for a sincere effort to improve performance when no tangible gains occur in certain time periods. Early success experiences build confidence and encourage continued experimenting.

   Don't ask people to do what they really are not capable of doing, thereby inviting a sense of failure. At the same time do provide the opportunity to learn, stretch and grow; to experience a sense of successful achievement.

6. In the early stages of change from an authoritative to a consultative or participative work structure, the team should have available all the resource-person help or guidance it may want. Either a resource person or a specially designated ombudsman should be readily available to the group in this transition stage.

   It is important that some appropriate structure be set up in the organization to assure sustained commitment to the team approach and to other concomitants of a job enrichment program. One way to achieve this might be to invite each major segment of the organization, such as sales, the key production components, accounting, quality assurance, etc., to nominate two volunteers to participate in a Steering Committee. One person from each major department might be a supervisor and one a nonsupervisor. Such an arrangement might add up to a group of about 10-14 persons who would constitute an internal voice to provide thrust, support, and nurture to the program as well as to monitor it. This group would maintain self-development in their knowledge about quality of worklife improvement and bring in new ideas from the outside. For example, they might make contact with other companies in the region operating in a similar management style, attend occasional workshops or courses related to quality of worklife and productivity improvement, etc.

A related requirement is to provide an excellent ongoing internal training program, both for refresher purposes and to orient groups of new employees in the philosophy and practice of this style of management. Such training (which has been referred to in point #5) can be led by a competent internal training officer, or by a knowledgeable consultant working in tandem with the inside staff. This training is needed to support the efforts of the Steering Committee referred to above.

A word of warning to any outside consultant: he should minimize any credit ascribed to him by management if the program progresses successfully. His stance should never imply that his help is anything more than facilitator, catalyst, resource person or perhaps occasional gadfly for getting the organization's personnel to work more effectively together in identification and constructive resolution of their problems/opportunities.

7. Time should be set aside for a periodic post-mortem by all concerned. "How are we doing?" and "What changes or modifications in policy or procedure might we like to try to overcome problems, make further improvement?" are questions that should be discussed by those concerned.

8. Top management of the organization—or at least of the division involved—should give recognition and reward (positive reinforcement) for any unusual noteworthy accomplishment by a task group. This is in addition to the day-by-day recognition noted in point #5.

9. Any persistent problems in the operation should be studied by all concerned. The atmosphere here should be problem solving and not culprit seeking.

10. After the change has been in operation for a year or two, surveys should be made at regular intervals to find any problems or suggestions which have not come to light through the everyday communication channels provided. Such sur-

veys are best made through confidential, open-ended interviews conducted by someone the members trust—perhaps (but not necessarily) an outside consultant.

11. If the group improves productivity, all members should share in these gains. Cost-savings sharing arrangements such as adaptations of the Scanlon Plan might be examined in depth.

As we have noted earlier, jealousy and dissension may result among workers who are not participating in the experiment if one segment of the organization—the experimental group—is drawing higher pay in any form from the productivity gains or from some different way of evaluating their pay grades. When success has been demonstrated and if the principles can be extended to the entire operation, this may be the ripe time to introduce cost-saving sharing with the entire work force.

NOTES

1. L. E. Davis, *The Design of Jobs*, Reprint No. 163 (Los Angeles: UCLA, Institute of Industrial Relations, 1966).

2. F. Herzberg, "One More Time: How Do You Motivate Employees?" *Harvard Business Review*, Jan.-Feb. 1968, 53-62.

3. E. Ginzberg, "The Humanizing of Europe's Assembly Lines," *World Magazine*, September 26, 1972, 22-26.

4. N. Herrick and M. Maccoby, "Humanizing Work: A Priority Goal of the 1970s," presented at the International Conference on the Quality of Working Life, Arden House, Harrison, NY, September 1972.

5. From his chapter in *The Worker and the Job*, pp. 173-174.

6. Technical Report No. 3, Department of Administrative Sciences, Yale University, May 1974.

7. Edward Glover and Associates is a firm of psychological consultants.

Enriching Jobs and Installing Changes

The material in this chapter is based on "Improving the Quality of Worklife Work Design," prepared for the U.S. Department of Labor by J. Richard Hackman, Yale University, and published as PB 255 044, June 1975.

PRINCIPLES FOR ENRICHING JOBS

Core job dimensions are directly tied to a set of action principles for redesigning jobs. As shown in the figure, these principles specify what types of changes in jobs are most likely to lead to improvements in each of five core job dimensions, and thereby to an increase in the overall motivating potential of the job as a whole.

ACTION PRINCIPLES FOR CHANGING JOBS

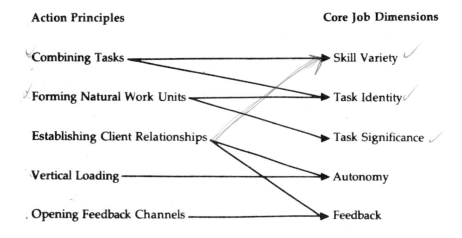

Action Principles	Core Job Dimensions
Combining Tasks	Skill Variety
Forming Natural Work Units	Task Identity
Establishing Client Relationships	Task Significance
Vertical Loading	Autonomy
Opening Feedback Channels	Feedback

Forming Natural Work Units

A critical step in the design of any job is the decision about how the work is to be distributed among the people who do it. Numerous considerations affect that decision, such as technological constraints, level of worker training and experience, "efficiency" from an industrial or systems engineering perspective, and equity of individual workloads. Work designed on the basis of these factors usually is distributed among employees rationally and logically. The problem is that the logic used does not include the needs of employees for personally meaningful work.

Consider, for example, a typing pool (consisting of one supervisor and ten typists) that handles all work for one division of a company. Jobs are delivered in rough draft or dictated form to the supervisor, who distributes them as evenly as possible among the typists. In such circumstances the individual letters, reports, and other tasks performed by a given typist in one day or week are randomly assigned. There is no basis for identifying with the work or the person or department for whom it is performed, or for placing any personal value upon it.

By contrast, creating natural units of work increases employee "ownership" of the work, and therefore improves the chances that they will view it as meaningful and important rather than as irrelevant and boring.

In creating natural units of work, one must first identify what the basic work items are. In the typing pool example, that might be "pages to be typed." Then these items are grouped into natural and meaningful categories. For example, each typist might be assigned continuing responsibility for all work requested by a single department (or by several smaller departments). Instead of typing one section of a large report, the individual will type the entire piece of work, with knowledge of exactly what the product of the work is. Furthermore, over time the typist will develop a growing sense of how the work affects co-workers or customers who receive the completed product. Thus, as shown in the figure, forming natural units of work increases two of the core job dimensions that contribute to experienced meaningfulness: task identity, and task significance.

It is still important that work be distributed so that the system as a whole operates efficiently, of course, and workloads must be arranged so that they are approximately equal among employees. The principle of natural work units simply requires that these traditional criteria be supplemented so that, insofar as possible, the tasks that arrive at an employee's work station form an identifiable and meaningful whole.

Combining Tasks

The very existence of a pool made up entirely of persons whose sole function is typing reflects a fractionalization of jobs that sometimes can lead to such hidden costs as high absenteeism and turnover, extra supervisory time, and so on. The principle of combining tasks is based on the assumption that such costs often can be reduced by simply taking existing and fractionalized tasks and putting them back together again to form a new and larger module of work. At the Medfield, Massachusetts plant of Corning Glass Works, for example, the job of assembling laboratory hotplates was redesigned by combining a number of previously-separate tasks. After the change, each hotplate was assembled from start to finish by one operator—instead of going through several separate operations performed by different people.

Combining tasks (like forming natural work units) contributes in two ways to the experienced meaningfulness of the work. First, task identity is increased. The hotplate assembler, for example, can see and identify with a finished product ready for shipment— rather than a nearly invisible junction of solder. Moreover, the more tasks that are combined into a single worker's job, the greater the variety of skills he must call on in performing the job. So, task combination also leads directly to greater skill variety, further increasing the meaningfulness of the work.

Establishing Client Relationships

Jobs designed according to traditional criteria often provide the worker with little or no contact with the ultimate user of his product or service. As a consequence, the worker may have difficulty generating high commitment and motivation to do the job well.

By establishing direct relationships between workers and their clients, jobs often can be improved in three ways. First, feedback increases because additional opportunities are created for the employee to receive direct praise or criticism of his work outputs. Second, skill variety may increase, because of the need to develop and exercise one's interpersonal skills in managing and maintaining the relationship with the client. Finally, autonomy will increase to the degree the individual is given real personal responsibility for deciding how to manage his relationships with the people who receive the outputs of his work.

Creating client relationships can be viewed as a three-step process: (a) identification of who the client actually is; (b) establishing the most direct contact possible between the worker and the client; and (c) establishing criteria and procedures so that the client can judge the quality of the product or service he receives and relay his judgments directly back to the worker. Especially important (and, in many cases, difficult to achieve) is identification of the specific criteria by which the work output is assessed by the client—and ensuring that both the worker and the client understand these criteria and agree with them.

Vertical Loading

In vertical loading, the intent is to partially close the gap between the "doing" and the "controlling" aspects of the job. Thus, when a job is vertically loaded, responsibilities and controls that formerly were reserved for management are added to the job. Among ways this might be achieved are the following:

Giving job incumbents responsibility for deciding on work methods, and for advising or helping train less experienced workers.

Providing increased freedom in time management, including decisions about when to start and stop work, when to take a break, and how to assign priorities.

Encouraging workers to do their own trouble-shooting and manage crises to the extent they feel is appropriate, rather than calling immediately for a supervisor.

Providing workers with increased knowledge of the financial aspects of the job and the organization, and increased control over budgetary matters that affect their own work.

When a job is vertically loaded, it inevitably increases in autonomy. As shown in the figure, this should lead to increased feelings of personal responsibility and accountability for the work outcomes.

Opening Feedback Channels

In virtually all jobs there are ways to open channels of feedback to individuals to help them learn whether their performance is improving, deteriorating, or remaining at a constant level. While there are various sources from which information about performance can come, it usually is advantageous for a worker to learn about his performance directly as he does his job—rather than from management on an occasional basis.

Job-provided feedback is more immediate and private than supervisor-supplied feedback, and increases the worker's feelings of personal control over his work in the bargain. Moreover, it avoids many of the potentially disruptive interpersonal problems which can develop when the only way a worker has to find out how he is doing is from direct messages or subtle cues from the boss.

Exactly what should be done to open channels for job-provided feedback varies from job to job and organization to organization. Yet in many cases the changes involve simply removing existing blocks which isolate the individual from naturally-occurring data about performance, rather than generating entirely new feedback mechanisms. For example:

Establishing direct relationships (discussed above) often removes blocks between the worker and natural external sources of data about his work.

Quality control efforts in many organizations often eliminate a natural source of feedback, because all quality checks are done by people other than the individuals responsible for the work. In such cases, feedback to the workers, if there is any, may be belated and diluted. By placing most quality control functions in the worker's own hands, the quantity and quality of data available to him about his own performance will dramatically increase.

Tradition and established procedure in many organizations

dictate that records about performance be kept by a supervisor and transmitted up (not down) the organizational hierarchy. Sometimes supervisors even check the work and correct any errors themselves. The worker who made the error never knows it occurred and is therefore denied the very information which can enhance both his internal work motivation and the technical adequacy of his performance. In many cases, it is possible to provide standard summaries of performance records directly to the worker (as well as to his superior), thereby giving him personally and regularly the data he needs to improve his effectiveness. -

Computers and other automated machines sometimes can be used to provide the individual with data now blocked from him. Many clerical operations, for example, are now performed on computer consoles. These consoles often can be programmed to provide the clerk with immediate feedback in the form of a CRT display or a print-out indicating that an error has been made. Some systems even have been programmed to provide the operator with a positive feedback message when a period of error-free performance has been sustained.

The principles for redesigning jobs reviewed here, while illustrative of the kinds of changes that can be made to improve the jobs of individuals in organizations, obviously are not exhaustive.

INSTALLING PLANNED CHANGES IN JOBS

Over the last two years numerous organizations have been visited where work redesign activities were being planned, implemented or evaluated. Large numbers of employees, managers, and internal and external consultants were talked with. In several cases, quantitative assessments have been made of the effects of work redesign projects.

What was seen is not encouraging. If these activities are representative, job enrichment projects are failing at least as often as they are succeeding. And the reasons for the failures, in many cases, appear to have more to do with the way planned changes are implemented in organizations than with the intrinsic merit of the changes themselves. Again and again good ideas about the redesign of work die because the advocates of change were unable to gain acceptance for their ideas, or because unexpected roadblocks led to early termination of the change project.

These observations are summarized below as six prescriptive guides for implementing changes in jobs. Each guide includes discussion of pitfalls that frequently were encountered in work redesign projects studied, as well as ingredients that were common to many of the more successful projects.

Guide 1: Diagnose the Work System Prior to Change

It is now reasonably clear that work redesign is not effective in all organizational circumstances. Yet rarely is a systematic diagnosis carried out beforehand to determine whether meaningful change is feasible, given the jobs being considered and the people who will be involved. As a result, faulty initial assumptions often go uncorrected, and the change project may be doomed before it is begun.

The choice of the job to be changed, for example, often appears near-random. Perhaps a manager will decide that a given job "seems right" for enrichment. Or he will settle on a job because it is peripheral to the major work done in the organization—thereby minimizing the risk of severe disruption if something should go wrong. Or a job will be selected because everything seems wrong with it: the work is not getting done on time or correctly; employees are furious about everything from their pay to the cleanliness of the restrooms; grievances are excessive; and so on. The hope, apparently, is that somehow redesigning the job will fix everything all at once.

It isn't so, of course. Some jobs, given existing technological constraints, are about as good as they ever can be—and work redesign in such cases is at best a waste of time. Other jobs have so much wrong with them (for example, engineering problems, poor supervision, inequitable pay) that job enrichment is totally irrelevant and could not conceivably bring about a noticeable improvement—indeed it might add even more complexity to an already-chaotic situation. When such matters are overlooked in planning for work redesign, the result often is a change effort that fails simply because it is aimed at an inappropriate target.

Similarly, differences in employee "readiness" to handle contemplated changes in jobs infrequently are assessed before a project is installed. Line managers often express doubts that employees can handle proposed new responsibilities, or skepticism that employees will enjoy working on an enriched job. Sometimes, as planning for work redesign proceeds, managers become convinced of the contrary. But only rarely are change projects designed with full cognizance of the fact that employees may differ in their psychological readiness for enriched work.

Even less frequently is explicit assessment made of the readiness of managers themselves to deal with the kinds of problems that inevitably arise when a major organizational change is made. In one case, the management team responsible for a job enrichment project nearly collapsed when the first serious change-related problem emerged. Time and energy that were needed for the project were spent instead working on intra-team issues that had been flushed out by the problem—and another "job enrichment failure" was added to the tally while the managers talked and talked. An adequate diagnosis of the readiness of the management team for management change would have increased the likelihood that the problematic intra-team issues would have been dealt with before the work redesign activities themselves were initiated.

The commitment of middle and top management to job enrichment also rarely received diagnostic attention in the observed organizations. Whether organizational change activities must begin at the top—or whether work redesign is a strategy for change that can spread from the bottom up—remains an important and unresolved question. It is almost always the case, however, that middle and top management can terminate a project they find unsatisfactory, whether for good reasons or on a whim. In one case, a high-level executive agreed to serve as "sponsor" for a project without really understanding what the changes would involve. When difficulties in implementation developed, the executive concluded that he had been misled—and the project found itself out from under its protective umbrella and in serious organizational jeopardy. In another case, a single vice-president was counted upon to project a fledgling project from "meddling" by others who favored alternative approaches to organizational change. When the vice-president departed the organization to attend a several-month executive development program, his temporary replacement terminated job enrichment activities and substituted a program more to his own liking. In both cases, an early assessment of the attitudes of key top managers would have revealed the need to develop a broader and better-informed base of high-level support for the project.

A number of organizations studied did conduct diagnoses of the work system before changes were installed, and almost invariably these studies identified problems or issues that required attention prior to the beginning of the job changes themselves. Here are some of the issues addressed in successful diagnoses observed:

> Can the jobs under consideration be meaningfully changed? That is, will work redesign make enough of a difference in the jobs to affect the people who do them? Would meaningful job changes involve unrealistically high expenditures of capital, or alteration of unalterable technology? What specific aspects of the work are especially problematic at present?

> If the jobs are open to meaningful change, what about the work is particularly problematic at present? What other aspects of the job might provide opportunities for change that could increase the level of self-motivation of employees in their work?

> Are the employees reasonably ready for change and capable of handling their new duties afterwards? Are they basically satisfied with bread-and-butter issues of pay, supervision, and job security—or would an attempt to improve jobs run into resistance and hostility because of existing dissatisfaction with these items? It is especially important to collect explicit, reliable data on such issues, because they are matters for which a relatively high level of misperception and stereotyping on the part of managers may be expected. In particular, managers often overestimate the present satisfaction of employees with the bread-and-butter issues, and underestimate employee's psychological readiness and technical competence to take on added responsibility and challenge in their work.

> Is management itself ready to handle the extra burdens and challenges that will be created by the change? Some management teams are not, and it is better to find out early than to risk a major breakdown early in the project.

> What aspects of the surrounding work system are likely to be

affected by the change (including both clients and holders of adjacent jobs)? Are these groups ready and able to handle the different demands that the change might bring, or is development work required with them prior to (or as part of) the change project? Will the change require problematic alteration of equipment or technical procedures?

Diagnoses that address such questions are not easy to make. They involve the raising of anxieties at a time when most participants in the project are instead seeking comfort and assurance that everything will turn out all right. Moreover, the tools and methodologies required for undertaking such diagnoses only now are beginning to become available. However, the diagnostic task itself may be one of the most crucial of all in a work redesign project.

Guide 2: Keep the Focus on the Work Itself

Redesigning a job often appears seductively simple. In practice, it is a rather challenging undertaking—requiring a good deal more energy than most other organizational development activities, such as attitude improvement programs, training courses, and objective-setting practices.

There are many reasons why it is hard to change jobs. At the purely bereaucratic level, the entire personnel-and-job-description apparatus often must be engaged to get the changes approved, documented, and implemented. If the organization is unionized, the planned changes often must be negotiated beforehand— sometimes a formidable task. Simple inertia often tempts managers to add lots of window dressing to make things appear different, rather than actually to change what people *do* on their jobs. Finally, when even one job in an organization is changed, many of the interfaces between that job and related ones must be dealt with as well. In even moderately complex work systems this is no small matter.

It is easy, apparently, for those responsible for work redesign activities to delude themselves about what is actually being altered in such projects, and thereby to avoid the rather difficult task of actually changing the structure of the work people do. One of the best ways of ensuring that a project stays focused on the work itself is to base change activities firmly on a theory of work design.

Some theories are doubtless better than others. Observations suggest, however, that the specific details of various theories may not be as important as the fact that *some* theory is used to guide the implementation of change. In addition to keeping the changes focused on the originally-intended objective of restructuring the work itself, a good theory can help identify the kinds of data needed to plan and evaluate the changes, and can alert implementors to special problems and opportunities that may develop as the project unfolds.

The theory must, however, be appropriate for the changes that are contemplated. Therein lies one of the major difficulties of the stock transfer project described later. The project was originally designed on the basis of motivation-hygiene theory, which deals exclusively with the enrichment of jobs performed by individuals. The changes that were actually made, however, involved the creation of enriched *group* tasks.

Because the theory did not address the special problems of designing work for groups (e.g., how to create conditions that encourage members to share with one another their special skills relevant to the group task), those responsible for implementation found the theory of limited use as a guide for planning and installing the changes. Gradually the theory dropped from their attention, and without the benefit of theory-specified guidelines for change the project became increasingly diffuse—eventually addressing many issues that had little or nothing to do with the work itself.

Guide 3: Prepare Ahead of Time for Unexpected Problems

When substantial changes are made in jobs, shock waves may be created that reverberate throughout adjacent parts of the organization. If insufficient attention is given to such "spin-off" effects of job changes, they may backfire and create problems that negate (or even reverse) hoped-for positive outcomes.

The site of the backfire varies from case to case. In one company, employees who prepared customer accounts for computer processing were given increased autonomy in scheduling their work and in determining their own work pace. This resulted in a less-predictable schedule of data input to the computer system. Because the data processing department had not been involved in the work redesign project, excessive computer delays were encountered while data processing managers struggled to figure out how to respond to the new and irregular flow of work. The net result was an increase in antagonism between computer operators and the employees whose jobs had been enriched—and a decrease in the promptness of customer service.

In another company, work was redesigned to give rank-and-file employees a number of responsibilities that previously had been handled by their supervisors. The employees (who dealt with customers of the company by telephone) were given greater opportunities for personal initiative and discretion in dealing with customers, and initially seemed to be prospering in their new responsibilities. But later observations revealed a deterioration in morale, especially in the area of supervisor-subordinate relationships. Apparently the supervisors had found themselves with little work to do after the change (the employees were handling much of what they had done before), and when they turned to higher management for instructions, they were told to "develop your people—that's what a manager's job is." The supervisors had little idea what "developing your people" involved, and in many cases implemented that instruction by standing over the employee's shoulders and correcting each error they could find. Resentment between the supervisor and the employee groups soon developed, and more than overcame any positive benefits that had accrued from the changes in the job itself.

The implication is clear: organizations are giving insufficient attention—both prior to the change, in planning activities, and afterwards—to the ways the change may affect other aspects of the workplace, and the result is often a "failure" of work redesign.

In many cases, such failures can be avoided by developing contingency plans ahead of time to deal with the spin-off problems that inevitably accompany changes in jobs. Contingency plans can be advantageous in at least two ways. First, employees, managers, and consultants all will share an awareness that problems are likely to emerge elsewhere in the work system as the change project develops. This simple understanding may help keep surprise and dismay at manageable levels when the problems do in fact appear, and thereby decrease the opportunity for people to conclude prematurely that "the project failed."

Second, pre-planning for possible problems can lead to an objective increase in the readiness of all parties to deal with the problems that do emerge. Having a few contingency plans filed away can lessen the chances that unexpected problems will get out of hand before they can be adequately dealt with—draining needed energy from the change project itself in the process.

Not all contingency plans can be worked out in detail beforehand. Indeed, they probably should not be, because until a project is underway one cannot know for sure what the specific nature of the most pressing needs and problems will be. But one can be ready to deal with common problems that may appear. For example, the training department can be alerted that some training may be required if managers find themselves in difficulty supervising the employees after the work is redesigned; those responsible for the reward system can be asked to engage in some contingency planning on the chance that the new work system may require nontraditional compensation arrangements; and so on. One does not begin with these matters, but one is well-advised to anticipate that certain of them will arise, and to be prepared to deal with them when and if they do.

Guide 4: Evaluate Continuously

When managers or consultants are asked whether or not a work redesign project has been evaluated, the answer nearly always is affirmative. But when one asks to see the evaluation, the response frequently is something like "Well, let me tell you. . .only one week after we did the actual job changes this guy who had been on the lathe for fifteen years came up me, and he said. . . ." Such anecdotes are interesting, but they provide little help to managers and union officials as they consider whether or not work redesign is something that should be experimented with further, and possibly diffused throughout the organization. Nor is it the stuff of which generalizable behavioral science knowledge is made.

Sometimes "hard" data are pointed to, often financial savings resulting from reductions in personnel in the unit where the work redesign took place. Such data can validly document an improvement in worker productivity, but they are of little value in understanding the full richness of what has happened, or why. And, of great importance in unionized organizations, they are hardly the kind of data that will engage the enthusiasm of the bargaining unit for broader application of work redesign.

There are many good reasons why adequate evaluations of work redesign projects are not done: not having the capability of translating human gains into dollars and cents; there being so many influences on measured productivity and unit profitability that it is hard to separate out what was due to the job changes; having an organization-wide accounting system that cannot handle the costs of absenteeism, turnover, training, and extra supervisory time; not really trusting measures of job satisfaction; and so on.

These reasons can be convincing, at least until one asks what was done to try to overcome the problems and gets as a response "Well, we really didn't think we could get the accounts to help out, so. . ." And one is left with several unhappy hypotheses: (a) nobody knows how to do a decent evaluation—nor how to get help in doing one; or (b) management does not consider systematic evaluation an essential part of the change activity; or (c) the desire of the people responsible for the program to have it appear successful is so strong that they cannot afford the risk of an explicit evaluation.

Because of the pressure on lower-level managers and consultants to make job enrichment programs at least appear successful, it often is necessary for top management or union leaders to insist that learningful evaluations of such programs take place. And for the evaluations to be valid and useful, management must attempt to create an organizational climate in which the evaluation is viewed as an occasion for learning—rather than as an event useful mainly for evaluating the performance and competence of those who actually installed the changes.

Such a stance permits interim disappointments and problems to be used as times for reconsideration and revision of the change project, rather than as a cause for disillusionment and abandonment. It encourages implementors to learn as they go how most effectively to design, install and manage enriched jobs—a matter of considerable importance, since there is no neat package for redesigning work in organizations and probably never will be.

Taking a "learning" orientation to work redesign is, however, a costly proposition. It is expensive to collect trustworthy data for use in monitoring a project throughout its life, and to actively experiment with different ways of changing jobs. It is painful to learn from failure, and to try again. Yet such costs may actually be among the better investments an organization contemplating work redesign can make—because paying them may be the only realistic way for the organization to develop the considerable knowledge and expertise it will need to reap the full benefits of work redesign as a strategy for change.

Guide 5: Confront the Difficult Problems Early

Individuals responsible for work redesign projects often find it tempting to get the project "sold" to management and union leadership, and only then to begin negotiations on the difficult problems that must be solved to actually carry out the project. This seems entirely reasonable: if such problems are raised before the project is agreed to, the chances are increased that it will never get off the ground. It appears, nevertheless, that in the long run it may be wiser to risk not doing a project for which the tough issues cannot be resolved beforehand than to do one under circumstances that require compromise after compromise to keep the project alive after it has begun.

Vigilance by those responsible for the change is required to ensure that the tough issues are not swept under the rug when the project is being considered. Among such issues (that too often are reserved for later discussion) are:

> The nature and extent of the commitment of management and union leaders, including the circumstances under which a decision may be made to terminate the project. Of special import is making sure that both management and union leadership realize that problems will emerge in the early stages of a project, and that a good deal of energy may be required to protect and nurture the project during such "down" phases.

The criteria against which the project ultimately will be evaluated and the means by which evaluation will be done, including measures that will be used. Given that there are serious measurement difficulties in assessing any work redesign project, it is important to make sure that all parties, including management and union sponsors, are aware of these difficulties and are committed at the outset to the evaluation methodology.

The way that learnings gained in the project (whether they be "successful tactics we discovered" or "roadblocks we unexpectedly encountered") will be made available to people who can use them as guides for future action. Especially critical are efforts to establish early a climate that encourages non-punitive discussion and analysis of the project as it develops.

Guide 6: Design Change Processes That Fit with the Change Objectives

Most work redesign projects provide employees with increased opportunities for autonomy and self-direction in carrying out the work of the organization. Employees are allowed to do their work with a minimum of interference, and are assumed to have the competence and sense of responsibility to seek appropriate assistance when they need it. The problem is that far too often the process of implementing job enrichment is strikingly incongruent with that intended end state.

It appears unrealistic to expect that a more flexible, bottom-loaded work system can be created using implementation procedures that are relatively rigid and bureaucratic, and that operate strictly from the top down. Yet again and again it was observed that standard, traditional organizational practices were used to install work redesign. More often than not employees were the last to know what was happening, and only rarely were they given any real opportunity to actively participate in and influence the changes. In many cases they were never told the reasons why the changes were being made. As one employee put it: "They're dictating to me again, but this time about how *I* should enjoy taking more responsibility for getting their work out."

What happens during the planning stages of a work redesign project is illustrative of such incongruence between means and ends.

Typically initial planning for work redesign (including decision-making about what jobs will be changed) is done privately by managers and consultants. Diagnostic work, if performed at all, is done using a plausible cover story—such as telling employees that they are being interviewed "as part of our regular program of surveying employee attitudes." (The rationale is that employee expectations about change should not be raised prematurely; the effect often is that suspicions are raised instead.) Eventually managers appear with a fully-determined set of changes that are installed in traditional top-down fashion. If employees resist and mistrust the changes, managers are surprised and disappointed. As one said: "I don't understand why they did not respond more enthusiastically. Don't they realize how we are going to make their work a lot more involving and interesting?" Apparently he did not see the lack of congruence between the goals being aspired to and the means, between "What we want to achieve" and "How we're going to do it."

As an alternative approach, managers might choose to be public and participative in translating from theory through diagnosis to the actual steps taken to modify jobs. Such an approach could be advantageous for a number of reasons:

1. To the extent that diagnostic data are collected and discussed openly, everyone who will be affected by the changes has the chance to become more involved in the redesign activities, more knowledgeable about them, and therefore less threatened by them. In one organization, managers initally were very skeptical about employee participation in planning for job changes. After employees had become involved in the project, however, a number of managers commented favorably on the amount of energy employees contributed to the planning activities, and on the constructive attitude they exhibited.

2. The quality of the diagnostic data themselves may be improved. If employees know that changes in their own work will be made partly on the basis of their responses to the diagnostic instruments, they may try especially hard to provide valid and complete data.

3. Chances are increased that learnings will emerge from the project that can be used to develop better action principles of

work redesign for future applications. The involvement of people from a diversity of organizational roles in diagnostic change-planning activities should facilitate attempts to piece together a complete picture of the change project—including the reasons that various changes were tried, what went wrong (and what went right), and what might be done differently next time.

4. Expectations about change indeed will be increased when employees are involved in diagnostic and change-planning processes. But rather than being something to be avoided, heightened employee expectations can serve as a positive force for change—for example, by countering the conservatism that inevitably creeps into changes planned and implemented downwards through several hierarchical levels in an organization.

Despite these potential advantages, it is not easy to carry off a fully participative work redesign project. Nor does openness and employee participation guarantee success. Indeed, some experienced commentators have argued explicitly against employee participation in planning job changes, because participation risks contaminating the change process with "human relations hygiene," because employees are not viewed as competent to redesign their own jobs, or because job design is viewed solely as a management function.

Observations of work redesign projects turned up few projects in which employee participation was actively used in the change process. And the ideas for change that employees proposed in these cases focused mainly on the removal of "roadblocks" from the work and on the improvement of hygiene items. This is consistent with the predictions that employee suggestions usually deal more with the context of work than with its motivational core.

The circumstances under which employees participated in work redesign activities in these organizations, however, were far from optimal. Often employees were simply asked "What would you suggest?" and given little time to consider their response. In no case were employees provided with education in the theory and strategy of job redesign before being asked for suggestions. And in all cases studied, employees had no real part in the final decision-making about what changes actually would be made. They were contributors to the change process, but not partners in it.

To develop and utilize the full potential of employees as resources for change would be an exciting undertaking, and a major one. It would require teaching employees the basics of motivation theory, discussing with them state-of-the-art knowledge about the strategy and tactics of work redesign, and providing them with training and experience in planning and installing organizational innovations.

Such an approach would be costly, perhaps too much so to be practical. But it would have the advantage of encouraging employees to become full collaborators in the redesign of their own work, thereby creating a process for improving jobs that is consistent with the ultimate objectives of the change. Moreover, and of special importance to the quality of worklife in organizations, the approach would provide employees with greatly increased opportunities for furthering their own personal growth and development—and at the same time significantly increase their value as human resources within the organization.

Learning from a
Failed Enrichment Program

The material in this chapter is based on "A Failure of Job Enrichment: the Case of the Change That Wasn't," prepared for the Manpower Administration, Office of Naval Research, by Linda L. Frank and J. Richard Hackman, Yale University, and published as AD-A007 356, March 1975.

Advocates of job enrichment as a strategy for organizational change have been living through a time of excitement. As originally formulated, job enrichment was seen primarily as a device for increasing the motivation, productivity, and satisfaction of people at work. Now, as reports of its success are multiplying, job enrichment is being acclaimed by some as a cure for problems ranging from inflation to drug abuse.

Others are finding reasons for skepticism about the technique. Reports of "job enrichment failures," while almost never published in management or scientific journals, are now beginning to circulate among operating managers and organizational development professionals. We believe it is unfortunate that systematic accounts and analyses of such failures are not more widely available—for at least two reasons.

First (and most importantly), it is through failure that we often learn the most about the strengths and weaknesses of behavioral science techniques—and discover previously unknown factors which must be accounted for in their implementation. Secondly, many managers and practitioners seeking ways to fix organizational problems never get alerted to the pitfalls associated with the change strategy they choose. As a consequence, they proceed to implement the strategy as if they were the first ever to use it, un-warned by the unreported failures of others, and unarmed against the problems in implementation they are sure to face.

The numerous reported successes of job enrichment as a change technique make a convincing case that the redesign of work can, in the right circumstances, significantly improve both the satisfac-tion of individual employees and the productive effectiveness of organizational units. The problem is to determine what the "right circumstances" are—and how to bring them about.

The following study, by documenting and analyzing the reasons for a seemingly clear *failure* of job enrichment, attempts to show how the success of work redesign interventions can be critically affected both by the nature of the changes themselves—and by the characteristics of the larger socio-technical system where the changes are installed.

THE RESEARCH SETTING

The Stock Transfer Department

The work redesign project was carried out in the stock transfer de-partment of a large metropolitan bank. The department is respon-sible for two distinct operations in changing the ownership of securities. The first is the legal transfer of securities from one owner to another: old stock certificates are destroyed, and new ones are issued to the new owner. Second, the change of owner-ship is officially recorded on the books of the corporation in-volved.

To remain competitive with stock transfer operations in other banks, the entire transfer process must be completed within forty-eight hours. Department employees perform sixteen different functions, many of which are directly involved with the operation of a data processing system. The computer system prints new stock certificates, files changes in ownership, and maintains vari-ous kinds of records. At the time of the research, about 300 em-ployees worked in the stock transfer department.

The Focal Jobs

The change project involved employees who worked on the six most central jobs in the department:

1. Preparation clerk. Sorts and tickets incoming securities.
2. Processor. Checks certificates to ensure that they have the proper signature guarantees, transfer taxes, assignments from brokers, etc.
3. Operator. Types the names and addresses of stock transferees on a console for processing by the computer.
4. Legal clerk. Deals with all questions relating to the law—e.g., death inheritance taxes, verification of testamentary letters, affidavit domiciles, and corporate resolutions.
5. Correction clerk. Corrects errors made by operators and processors, answers outside inquiries from customers, and checks incorrectly delivered stock, confirmations, and billings.
6. Typist. Types and mails all correspondence, such as notifications to clients of corrections which have been made.

Eighty-five percent of employees working on the focal jobs were female. Their mean age was 33, and their modal educational level was a high school degree.

Supervision and Management

Each employee in the department reported to a "work coordinator" (first-line supervisor) who was responsible for eight to twelve employees who performed the same work function. The work coordinators reported to one of four second-line managers. These four managers, headed by a vice-president in charge of operations, formed the "management team" of the stock transfer department. The vice-president reported to the executive vice-president in charge of the entire corporate trust division of the bank.

Consultants and Staff

Line managers in the stock transfer department were advised on personnel issues (including matters of employee morale, training programs, and work design) by two members of the bank personnel staff. At times personnel staff members were assisted in conceiving and carrying out change projects by outside consultants who were contracted for by the corporate personnel department.

THE CHANGE PROJECT

The idea for the job enrichment project originated with the corporate personnel department of the bank. For a number of months the staff of the personnel department had been watching for an appropriate site for a job enrichment project. The executive vice-president for corporate trust also had expressed a long-standing interest in job enrichment and other behavioral science interventions. When signs of employee dissatisfaction and work inefficiency (e.g., excessive overtime) were detected in the stock transfer department, the executive vice-president contracted with the corporate personnel officer to explore the possibility of undertaking a work redesign project within that department.

An external consultant (who had been meeting periodically with the personnel officer) was invited to meet with management and staff members in the stock transfer department, and a series of workshops was held for department managers about job enrichment and its implementation. After about three months, a concrete design for a job enrichment project within the department was formulated.

The basic plan was to create ten to thirteen "modules" within the department each of which would be a "miniature stock transfer department" in its own right. Each module would have its own work coordinator (supervisor), and would function as a semi-autonomous work group. The modules would have complete responsibility for a specific group of corporations whose stock was handled by the bank—in contrast to the previous arrangement where workers arbitrarily handled whatever work happened to be channeled their way by a supervisor.

Each module was to include one preparation clerk, two processors, six operators, one legal clerk, one correction clerk, and one typist. They were each to learn and eventually perform all of the functions in the module, thereby increasing the skills of the individual employees, the variety of their work, and the flexibility of the module as a whole. In addition, some of the specific jobs in the module were to be given additional "enriching" tasks.

It was hoped that the assignment of a specific set of corporations to each module would increase the workers' identification with and commitment to their work. These feelings of identification were to be strengthened by allowing workers in the module to leave work together when the security transactions from "their" companies had been handled (rather than with other employees who performed the same work function, as previously).

Furthermore, members of each module were to be provided with increased knowledge of the results of their work activities, through three new feedback mechanisms which were to be built into the modules. These were: (a) the presence of the corrections clerk in the module on a continuous basis, to immediately show members when they had made a mistake and to help them correct it; (b) the pairing of experienced operators with those less experienced, so the former could verify the latter's work; and (c) programming of the data processing system to provide individualized reports of performance to module members on a weekly basis.

The module was to be managed by the work coordinator, who would be trained sufficiently broadly that she could competently advise and supervise all the workers in the module—in effect, manage her own small stock transfer department.

It was expected that the modular operation would produce a general increase in the overall quality of the working experience and the work satisfaction of stock transfer workers. In addition, it was hoped there would be a reduction in work flow delays (because of the increased flexibility of the module) and an increase in the quality of service provided (because of the additional feedback provided to module members and because of increased employee commitment to the work).

Implementation Plan

Modules were scheduled to be introduced one at a time, with a six-week interval between the start of each one. Since the first module was set to begin before employees in that module could be cross-trained, it was decided to train these employees (including their work coordinator) after the system had been introduced and things had settled down. The remaining workers (i.e., those not scheduled to be in the first module) would be cross-trained before entering their modules. The three new feedback channels (i.e., direct input from correction clerks, pairing of operators for work verification, and computerized feedback of performance) were scheduled to be instituted immediately after Module One was begun.

Corporations were to be assigned to each module so that the number of securities to be processed would approximate the quantity done by a similar number of employees prior to the change. The appropriate quantity could not be computed with certainty, so it was decided to deliberately under-load Module One at the outset, and gradually increase the workload as the work capacity of the module became clear through experience.

One member of the management team was assigned major responsibility for supervising the modules—both as they were introduced, and after they were functioning. He was relieved of many of his previous duties so that he would have ample time to manage the change process.

THE EVALUATION PROJECT

Evaluation of the change project took place about five weeks after the first module had been introduced, just prior to the start of the second module. The research design specified that data would be collected just after each module had been installed. At those times data would be obtained not only from members of the newly-formed module, but also from employees working in previously-created modules (to assess the long-term effects of the change) and from employees who had not yet become part of a module (to assess any possible effects of history on the work group as a whole).

Three types of data were to be collected: (a) quantitative data on the nature of the jobs themselves and the reactions of employees to their jobs, using a standardized questionnaire; (b) quantitative data on employee performance effectiveness and absenteeism, drawing both on company records and supervisory ratings; and (c) qualitative data on the change process and its effects, from interviews with employees and managers, and from on-site observations. The researchers were to have no involvement in the change process itself, and were not to feed back data or findings until all changes were completed or the project was terminated by mutual agreement.

FINDINGS: QUANTITATIVE ANALYSES

Relationships Between Job Characteristics and Outcome Measures

Before examining the effects of the change to work modules on the jobs of stock transfer employees (and on their reactions to the newly-defined jobs) it is necessary to establish that the job characteristics which were measured in the research do in fact relate to the work attitudes and behavior of the employees. The theory from which the research questionnaire was derived specifies that the job dimensions measured (summarized by the Motivating Potential Score) should relate positively to employee satisfaction, motivation, work performance and attendance.

Correlations between MPS and these outcome variables for employees in the stock transfer department were made. All correlations were in the predicted direction, and many were of substantial magnitude.

These findings suggest that the job characteristics measured in the research were, in fact, good indicators of the degree to which a job would motivate and satisfy employees, and lead them to perform effectively and come to work regularly. Therefore, the measured job characteristics appeared to be appropriate for use as indicators of the "success" of the change to work modules within the stock transfer department of the bank.

Measured job characteristics and affective reactions were as follows:

Job Characteristics	**Affective Reactions**
Skill Variety	General Satisfaction
Task Identity	Internal Work Motivation
Task Significance	Specific Satisfaction:
Autonomy	Working Conditions
Feedback from the Job	Pay and Benefits
Feedback from Agents	Opportunities for
Dealing with Others	Growth

Effects of the Change on the Jobs and the People

Five separate sets of questionnaire data were obtained: (1) employees in Module One, after the change (October); (2) employees in Module Two prior to the change (October); (3) employees in Module One, long-term follow-up (March); (4) employees in Module Two, after the change (March); and (5) employees who were still working under the old system—i.e., whose jobs had not been changed at all (March).

Three sets of planned comparisons were computed for each of the dependent measures listed above. The comparisons, and results obtained, were as follows:

1. Comparison of Module One employees after the change with Module Two employees prior to the change (both sets of data collected in October). No significant effects were obtained for any of the dependent measures.

2. Comparison of Module Two employees prior to the change (October) with the same employees after the change (March). One comparison was statistically significant: Module Two employees experienced less Task Identity after the change to work modules than they had before.

3. Comparison of employees who were still working under the old system with Module One and Two employees (averaged). These data were all collected in March, and provide the most general test of employees who were in modules vs. those who were not. Comparisons were statistically significant for three of the measures of job characteristics, and in each case the employee in modules scored *lower* than did employees working under the former work system. The three measures were: Skill Variety, Feedback from the Job, and

Dealing with Others. No significant differences were obtained for any of the measures of employee affective reactions to their work.

In sum, these results suggest that the change to work modules had almost no impact on the characteristics of the jobs on which stock transfer employees worked. Indeed, the few statistically significant results obtained were in the "wrong" direction—i.e., jobs tended to get worse rather than better after the change to work modules. A similar pattern was encountered upon measuring employees' reactions to their work: Module Two employees were lower on almost all measures in March, after the change, than they were prior to the change. Moreover, Module One employees tended to score lower on the dependent measures in March (seven months after the change) than they did in October (one month after the change)—even though the October scores themselves were relatively low in comparison to those of employees who at that time were working under the old work system.

FINDINGS: WHAT ACTUALLY HAPPENED

It is tempting to conclude from the findings reported above that "job enrichment didn't work" in the stock transfer department. Indeed, exactly that conclusion was reached at the end of the project by several managers who had been involved in it. Such a conclusion is severely misleading, however, because the data show that the jobs themselves actually changed very little. To ask about the effects of enriched jobs in such circumstances is to ask an empty question. Instead, the critical issues in this project have to do with the reasons why the jobs were not substantially changed in the stock transfer department—and why those organizational changes that were carried out had no positive impact on employee attitudes or work behavior. These matters are examined below.

The Process of Implementation

The first module was implemented for the most part as planned. Operators were given some additional tasks to perform (such as classifying and checking the types of stock they were working with, and verifying the work of other operators). Legal and correction clerks were separated from colleagues who performed like functions, and joined the module. But neither the computer-based feedback system nor cross-training of employees was installed when the module was begun. As the time to implement Module Two approached, these innovations still had not been introduced; nevertheless, it was decided to proceed with Module Two on schedule.

The workload originally assigned to Module One turned out to be less than the capacity of module members. Therefore, management assigned Module Two twice the amount of work that had been given to the first module, to test the upper limit of module capacity. It was expected that after a few weeks of experience with Module Two the workload in both modules could be adjusted to a near-optimal level.

Shortly after the start of the second module, the data processing system began to malfunction with a frequency that was clearly debilitating to the entire department. A new set of programs for handling stock transfers had recently been installed, and "bugs" in the system were both more frequent and more disruptive to the operation of the department than had been anticipated. The result was that operators often had to remain idle for several hours during the day, and then were required to work overtime to compensate for the lost time. The computer difficulties continued, and by the third month of operation of Module Two, employees were putting in eight times as many overtime hours as they had the month Module One was instituted. Moreover, the manager who was primarily responsible for overseeing the installation and operation of the modules found it necessary to spend a substantial portion of his own time trying to get the computer system working. Soon members of the management team were embroiled in philosophical and logistical conflicts about departmental priorities.

The situation was further aggravated by the onset of the Christmas season, with its accompanying work holidays and increased workload. During the most difficult periods, many part-time employees were brought into the modules to help get the work done. This remedy did provide needed manpower, but also tended to undermine the integrity of the modules as self-contained units.

Shortly after the holiday season, the executive vice-president (who had been instrumental in the initiation and follow-through of the project) left the bank for a several month executive development program at a distant university. His temporary replacement was skeptical about the basic philosophy of job enrichment, preferring an alternative behavioral science approach to organizational change. At about the same time, the contract of the external consultant to the project expired—although he continued to visit the bank to discuss the project with members of the management team.

After the departure of the vice-president, the management team decided to delay the start of any additional modules until the problems with the first two were straightened out. Legal and correction clerks were removed from the modules and returned to their original work groups, where they could be supported by other people doing similar work. Neither cross-training nor the computer-based feedback system had been installed, and no initiatives were visible toward getting these activities underway. As the researchers left the bank, it was officially unclear whether the first two modules would be re-constituted—or whether additional modules eventually would be created—but the informal word was pessimistic about such prospects.

Impact of the Change Process on the Jobs

The summary Motivating Potential Score (MPS) was found to relate positively to desired personal and organizational outcomes for employees in the stock transfer department. And, as designed, installation of the semi-autonomous modules should have improved employees' jobs on at least four of the dimensions that contribute to measured MPS. Given that such improvements did not occur, it may be instructive to examine "what went wrong" for each of the core job characteristics.

Skill variety: This aspect of the work should have been substantially affected by the cross-training scheduled to take place among module members. But because cross-training never took place, workers in modules wound up utilizing about the same range and level of skill in their work as previously. While operators were given some additional tasks to do, the impact of these new duties on the job as a whole (and on their reactions to their work) was not great. Operators reported in interviews that their jobs had "felt different" shortly after the change to modules, but that it seemed to be mostly "the same old thing, just more work" after the new tasks had been learned.

Task identity: Since each module was to be assigned certain corporations for processing on a permanent basis, it was expected that module members would come to experience the entirety of the stock transfer task for those corporations as collectively "theirs." Thus, even though no individual module member would be performing the whole job at any given time, task identity at the group level would be expected to increase.

In fact, the data show a slight decrease in task identity as a result of the change—apparently because the boundaries of the modules were excessively permeable and under-structured. For example:

> When there was an overload of work for the corporations assigned to a module (a frequent occurrence for Module Two), some of that work would be distributed by management to other employees on the floor.

> Conversely, if workers in a module finished their own tasks, they often were required to assist others outside the module who had unfinished work.

> Temporary workers often were rotated through the modules.

> Module workers typically left work with others in their functional specialty rather than with other members of the module.

> The work coordinators were not fully trained in all functional specialties in the modules; therefore, employees frequently found it necessary to return to their original sections when they needed assistance on a work-related problem.

For all these reasons, employees continued to experience themselves more as functional specialists than as members of an interdependent group with a whole and identifiable group task. In this retrospective context, the failure to find an increase in task identity as a result of the change is not at all surprising.

Task significance: Since the stock transfer jobs were high in task significance to begin with, there was no attempt on the part of management to increase the workers' sense of task significance as part of the plan for the work modules. It is not surprising, therefore, that there were no substantial changes in the task significance of the jobs as a result of the creation of the modules.

Autonomy: It was planned that employees would experience more autonomy in the modules than they had previously, because each module would be an autonomous "miniature stock transfer department" making its own decisions about how and when to carry out various tasks. In fact, however, no structural alterations were provided to either require or encourage module members to take real responsibility for the corporations that they had been assigned. Moreover, members of management continued to give specific individuals within the modules specific work assignments, and to intervene whenever there was a work crisis. In effect, management retained the "real" responsibility for getting the work out. And employees wound up feeling about the way they had before joining the modules—namely, that they had very little "say" or autonomy in planning and carrying out their work.

Feedback from the job: The original plan for the modules specified that feedback would be increased within the modules via several different mechanisms (i.e., operator-verifier pairings, computer-based feedback, and increased interaction between correction clerks and other module members). Because of unanticipated pressures on management, the structural changes that would have been necessary to actually get such feedback mechanisms operative and functioning as intended were never made. The net effect was no increase in the feedback module members received about their individual or unit effectiveness.

LEARNINGS FROM THE FAILURE

Guide 1. Work redesign projects should be based on theory— and such theory should be congruent with the kinds of changes that are contemplated.

Most work redesign projects, if grounded in theory at all, tend to be based either on the motivator-hygiene theory of Frederick Herzberg or, less frequently, on some version of socio-technical systems theory. The reason is simply that, until recently, these two paradigms have been about the only ones available for guiding work redesign activities. Now, however, a number of alternative conceptual approaches to work redesign have begun to appear—some of which specify explicit "principles" for improving jobs. As a result, the knowledgeable practitioner currently has considerable choice about the conceptual approach he will take in planning a work redesign project.

Although some theories may be objectively "better" than others, observations suggest that the specific details of various theories may not be as importnat as the fact that some theory is used to guide the implementation of change—and to keep change activities focused on the intended objectives. Moreover, a good theory can help identify and specify the kinds of data needed in planning and evaluating the changes, and can alert implementors to special problems and opportunities that may develop as the project unfolds.

But the theory must be appropriate for the kinds of changes that are contemplated. Therein lies one of the major difficulties of the present change effort. While the stock transfer project was originally developed on the basis of one theoretical approach (the Herzberg motivator-hygiene theory), that theory focuses exclusively on the enrichment of individual jobs. And the stock transfer project, of course, had primarily to do with the creation of enriched group tasks (i.e., the work of semi-autonomous modules)—although it was anticipated that individual jobs within the modules would be substantially enriched as well.

At least two major difficulties developed because the theory used did not address the particular problems of designing work for interacting groups. First, because those responsible for implementation found the theory of limited use as a guide for planning and installing the changes, the theory gradually dropped from their attention. And, without the benefit of theory-specified guidelines for change, the project became increasingly diffuse in focus—eventually emphasizing many matters that had little or nothing to do with the work itself.

Secondly, because there were no conceptual guidelines to point out the importance of group-level phenomena to the success of the project, many critical interpersonal issues were never recognized or seriously considered. For example, the plan for module members to cross-train one another required significant interaction between older and younger employees for the first time, and required that some individuals share their own "special" expertise with individuals they perceived as having little to offer in return. Because such interpersonal issues were not addressed, the degree to which some of the planned changes could actually be implemented was impaired—and the impact of other changes (that were "officially" introduced) was seriously compromised.

Guide 2. An explicit diagnosis of the target jobs and of the surrounding social and technical systems should be carried out before the changes are initiated.

The results of the stock transfer experiment suggest that, at minimum, the following questions might usefully be asked in prechange diagnoses:

1. Can the jobs under consideration be meaningfully changed—i.e., can job enrichment make enough of a difference in the jobs to have a measurable impact on the people who do them? And if the jobs are open to meaningful change, which specific aspects of the work are particularly problematic at present? Some jobs in the stock transfer department (e.g., legal clerks) probably were about as good as they could be at the start of the job enrichment project; the change to create work modules, if it had been effective, probably would have stripped some of the richness from the work already being done by some people. Other jobs had enormous room for improvement—but the specific changes planned for those jobs were developed more from managerial intuition than from a systematic diagnosis of the work.

2. Are the employees reasonably ready for change and capable of handling their new duties afterwards? Are they generally satisfied with bread-and-butter issues of pay, supervision, and job security—or would an attempt to improve jobs run into resistance because of high existing dissatisfaction with such items? Unless employees' basic needs are satisfied, job enrichment—even if well-designed—may

not work. In the project reported here, these matters did not have much of a chance to compromise the reactions of employees to their new jobs—because the work itself did not change substantially. However, it is worth noting that a preliminary assessment of employee attitudes, skills, and satisfactions carried out as an input to planning for the change might have altered the content of the changes that were attempted and increased the chances that they would "take."

3. Is management itself ready to handle the extra burdens and challenges that will be created by the change? In the case given, external problems encountered in attempting to institute the job changes appeared to raise significant conflicts and difficulties among members of the management team charged with implementation—problems that apparently had been just below the surface before the project was begun. Retrospective analysis suggests that if a diagnosis of the internal dynamics of the management team had been carried out prior to the project, some of the intra-team issues could have been dealt with in a way that would have increased the team's readiness to deal with the significant external challenges it subsequently had to face.

4. What is the nature and extent of the commitment of top management to the change project? As noted earlier, in the stock transfer experiment, only a single vice-president was strongly committed to the project—and when he left (albeit temporarily), support for the project at higher levels vanished and the very survival of the project was jeopardized. If pre-change assessment of the commitment of upper management to the project had been made, educational activities might have been undertaken to develop a stronger and broader base of informed support for the experiment.

5. What other aspects of the surrounding work system are likely to be affected by the change (including both clients and holders of adjacent jobs)? Are these groups ready and able to handle the different demands that the change might bring, or is developmental work required with them prior to (or as part of) the change project? Will the change require problematic alteration of equipment or technical

procedures? In the present case, some planned changes in the focal jobs were found to be impractical because they created "interface problems" with surrounding units (especially the computer system). An unfortunate side-effect was that managerial energy constantly was being diverted from crisis to crisis—and little remained for the crucial developmental work required to get the job enrichment project off the ground and functioning.

Diagnoses that address such questions are not easy to make. They involve the raising of anxieties at a time when most participants in the project are instead seeking comfort and assurance that everything will turn out all right. Moreover, the tools and methodologies required for undertaking such diagnoses only now are beginning to become available. But observations of the stock transfer experiment suggest that the diagnostic task itself may be one of the most crucial of all in a job enrichment project.

Guide 3. Contingency plans should be prepared ahead of time to deal with the inevitable "spin-off" problems and opportunities that emerge from work redesign activities.

By making explicit contingency plans for dealing with possible problems, at least two advantages accrue. First, employees, managers, and consultants all will be well aware (and share the awareness) that certain types of problems (e.g., tension in superior-subordinate relationships; technical problems; coordination difficulties at the interfaces of work systems, and so on) are likely to emerge as the change project develops. This simple understanding may help keep surprise and dismay at manageable levels when the problems do in fact appear, and thereby decrease the opportunity for people to conclude prematurely that "it failed."

Second, pre-planning for possible problems can lead to an objective increase in the readiness of all parties to deal with those problems that do emerge. It is true that what can go wrong in an organizational change project often does, usually at the worst possible moment. Therefore, having a few contingency plans filed away can lessen the chances that unexpected problems will get out of hand before they can be adequately dealt with—draining needed energy from the change project itself in the process.

Clearly, the success of the stock transfer project was negatively affected by the lack of contingency plans for dealing with predictable problems. As noted earlier, insufficient diagnostic work was carried out to identify possible problem areas, which made contingency planning near-impossible in any case. But little preparation was made beforehand to deal even with those problem areas that were anticipated. For example, it was known prior to the start of the changes that systematic cross-training of employees in the modules would be needed so that they could switch from task to task and efficiently complete the work of the module as a whole. Yet even as employees actually began working in the modularized work system no training procedures had been developed. Similarly, although it was anticipated that there would be problems in identifying the appropriate workload for the modules, no workload measurement system for modularized work was ever devised.

Not all contingency plans can be worked out in detail beforehand. Indeed, they probably should not be, because until a project is under way one cannot know for sure what the specific nature of the most pressing need and problems will be. But one can be ready to deal with common problems that may appear. For example, the training department can be alerted that some training may be required if managers find themselves in difficulty supervising the employees after the work is redesigned; those responsible for the reward system can be asked to engage in some contingency planning on the chance that the new work system may require non-traditional compensation arrangements; and so on. To recapitulate: one does not begin with these matters; but one is well-advised to anticipate that certain of them will arise, and to prepare to deal with them when and if they do.

Guide 4. Those responsible for work redesign projects should anticipate setbacks, and be prepared for continuous evaluation and revision of action-plans throughout the project.

Given the inevitability of problems and crises in work redesign projects, it often is tempting for employees, managers and consultants to use the occasion of a problem that seems especially serious to abandon the project as a "failure." An often-effective antidote to such tendencies is for the central figures in a change project to adopt a view of the project that legitimizes learning as an important outcome of the project. Such a stance permits interim disappointments and problems to be used as an occasion for reconsideration and revision of the content and approach of the change project, rather than as a time for disillusionment and abandonment. This may be especially important for projects involving work redesign, because as yet there is no neat "package" available for installing job enrichment; indeed, there may never be any such package. As a consequence, it seems essential that implementors will have to learn as they go how most effectively to design, implement, and manage enriched jobs in their own organizations.

To effectively take a "learning" orientation to work redesign projects, however, requires that trustworthy data be collected and used to monitor and evaluate the project throughout its life. Without data that can be trusted, it will be difficult for those responsible for the project to test and revise their own perceptions of how things are going.

In the stock transfer project, for example, it was agreed to keep the collected research and evaluation data confidential. As a consequence, those who were deciding "what to do next" did not know that the work itself had not been significantly changed, even though there was data in hand relatively early in the project suggesting that alterations in the jobs had not been very substantial. Similarly, the data provided early warning of other problems that subsequently contributed to the failure of the project. In the end, it was found that, in the interest of "clean" research, precisely those data that they most needed to steer the project back onto course was kept from the responsible individuals.

The costs of adopting an open, evaluating stance, a stance that allows learning from failures and problems as well as from success, are real and high. Still, such costs must be accepted because they can lead to important long-term gains in knowledge and expertise. They can also help generate understandings that other people in other organizations can use in planning their own work redesign activities. Perhaps most importantly, accepting the work and the pain of on-going evaluation may be the single best way to ensure the success of the change project itself.

Participative Management
and the Quality of Worklife

The material in this chapter is based on "Improving the Quality of Work Life Managerial Practices," prepared for the U.S. Department of Labor by George Strauss, and published as PB 255 047, June 1975.

Participation has been widely recommended as a means of improving the quality of worklife and of raising productivity. In theory, participation releases creative energies and provides workers with a sense of accomplishment. Thus it strengthens the path-goal relationship and also enhances the work environment. Furthermore, it is consistent with our ideas of equality, democracy, and individual dignity. As such, it offers a morally attractive solution to many of the problems of industrial life.

The following two case examples are illustrative of how participation can help increase the quality of worklife and productivity. The first example was developed under the Scanlon Plan, while the second was initiated by the employees themselves.

This first case involves a situation in which the Planning Department had an idea for the rearrangement of the machines and the use of a conveyor to facilitate certain transport problems. A blueprint was made and posted on the bulletin board, but the employees stated that they could not read the blueprint and that, therefore, they could make very few, if any, suggestions about the proposed plan. Consequently, a small-scale model or templet of what the layout would look like under the new plan was placed at a central location in the department.

One afternoon, a member of the planning group happened to be in the department and started discussing the proposed layout with a few of the employees. After he had criticized the proposal in a number of respects, a great many comments were made both by the foreman and by the employees. These comments were gathered together and a production committee meeting was held, attended by the Industrial Engineer responsible for the proposal. At this meeting the employees and the foreman joined together in strenuous criticism of the conveyor part of the plan. After about two and one-half hours' discussion, the committee agreed that the rearrangement of the machines would be beneficial but wanted the engineer to reconsider several aspects of the conveyor system.

About a week later, the committee agreed to a modified version of the conveyor system, with the understanding that it would be installed in such a manner that they could make changes fairly easily. Subsequently, the committee did make several changes, especially in the manning of the new system. The drastic revision in the department layout and the revised conveyor system are now accepted as an improvement by the workers and the foremen concerned and the productivity of the department has been increased by about 20 per cent.

Another example of participation, entered into without the fuss of calling it an "experiment," comes from the Institute of Industrial Relations at Berkeley. The Institute consists of faculty and professional staff, who spend their time in teaching, research, and various forms of community service—and hardworking clerical staff who keep the place going. The Director and Associate Directors have primary responsibilities in teaching departments and, in effect, have largely abdicated their roles as facilitators. As a consequence, work was often poorly coordinated and important meetings were scheduled at the same time, resulting in substantial overload. Although personnel practices were good by most standards, relatively little attention was given to career development.

A number of the staff met together fairly spontaneously to discuss these problems. Committees were established to deal with such issues as building maintenance, work scheduling, and supplies. A program of performance appraisal was introduced and an instructor invited to teach a course on how this worked. The supply committee investigated alternative forms of duplicating equipment and introduced new equipment which substantially saves on staff time at no great increase in cost. Measures were taken to insure better scheduling of events and to provide for work sharing during peak periods. The maintenance committee pressured the University Building Department to replace a leaking roof and to wash down the interior walls. A semimonthly paper was started, with a rotating editorship.

The facilitative activities (scheduling, planning, dealing with maintenance, etc.) described in the above two examples would normally have been initiated by management. In both cases, the work groups handled them much better themselves.

Participation typically takes less dramatic forms than the ones indicated above. In fact, many managers have been practicing a lot more participation than they realize. On a day-to-day basis, participation may occur in locker rooms, at coffee breaks, and when a few men and the foremen gather for beers after work. It may occur when two workers discuss how to do a job or one man gives another some tips on how to deal with quality control. It also occurs through de facto delegation when a foreman neglects to pay attention to an able worker, who then corrects a serious problem on his own. And finally, it may occur when the union steward and foreman discuss grievances or the workers unilaterally set production "bogies" or limitations on output.

WHAT PARTICIPATION MEANS

"Participation" is an overworked and somewhat imprecise term. In the European context, the term often refers to workers' participation in management, usually through formal mechanisms which permit workers' representatives to influence and even control decisions affecting the organization as a whole. In the United States, participation is chiefly thought of in terms of management style which permits subordinates the opportunity to make or at least influence decisions with regards to matters of importance to them, particularly with regard to how they do their work.

Even within the U.S. context, "participation" can take a variety of forms, each of which is effective under different conditions and for different reasons. Precision of analysis requires that the various forms be more carefully distinguished than is usually done. This is especially so because the evidence suggests that the shotgun approach to participation just won't work. It is not enough to try any old kind of participation on any old type of problem. Researchers and practitioners alike should use the small bore rifle (with telescopic sights) rather than the blunderbuss.

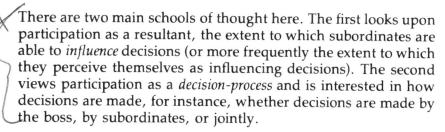

There are two main schools of thought here. The first looks upon participation as a resultant, the extent to which subordinates are able to *influence* decisions (or more frequently the extent to which they perceive themselves as influencing decisions). The second views participation as a *decision-process* and is interested in how decisions are made, for instance, whether decisions are made by the boss, by subordinates, or jointly.

The increased communications generated by the participation process leads to better ideas being expressed and this contributes to the quality of organizational decisions. But it is the feeling of influence that facilitates commitment to the decisions which are finally reached.

HOW PARTICIPATION WORKS

We know that participation—in some circumstances—has a positive effect on quality of worklife. The question is *how* and *when* this occurs. In other words, it is not enough to think of participation as a little black box into which participation is fed at one end and out of which higher production and satisfaction come at the other end. What happens within this box? What are the essential steps and the major variables within the participation process and how important is each?

Expectancy theory suggests that participation might lead to higher productivity if it contributes to workers preceiving that: (1) increased effort will lead to increased performance (productivity); (2) increased performance will lead to satisfaction of important needs (especially achievement and group acceptance); and (3) the satisfaction obtained from this effort is sufficiently great to make the effort worthwhile (the equity factor). Finally, participation may also affect the "psychological bargain" between the organization and its employees.

Participation Making It Easier to Convert Effort Into Performance

Participation may result in better and easier ways of doing the job being developed, so that a given degree of effort will result in higher performance. This may occur because the participative atmosphere permits subordinates to suggest and implement valuable new ideas which will make the organization more efficient. The participative atmosphere may also permit subordinates to question their boss's idea or to provide him with additional information which he can use in making decisions. Where participation occurs in a group, members may exchange ideas on how to improve performance. And practice in participation may lead to subordinates developing valuable new skills.

Whether participation of this sort can occur depends on a number of factors:

> (a) How much relevant information can the subordinate contribute?
>
> (b) Is the technology such that workers, individually or as a group, are in a position to change it? Meaningful suggestions are less likely to be forthcoming, for example, if the production process depends on costly machines which would be expensive to change.
>
> (c) Is there still "slack" in the sense that group discussion is likely to unearth significantly improved ways of doing things—or has the process been around for so long that most bugs have already been worked out?

Participation may help subordinates define their objectives and so direct their efforts more effectively. As discussed earlier, much organizational inefficiency and employee dissatisfaction derives from the fact that individuals aren't really quite sure what they are supposed to be doing. People are more likely to understand and accept goals which they set for themselves.

Participation, of course, can lead to greater team work.

Participation Making It More Likely That Performance Will Lead to Rewards

Participation may lead workers to believe that by working harder they will obtain (1) a sense of achievement and/or (2) a sense of social approval from their peers.

1. *Achievement:* A person is more likely to develop a sense of achievment of performing his job when the following conditions prevail:

> The individual has a generalized need for achievement.
>
> He feels that he has certain skills; for example, he is a good carpenter or is good at deciding how carpentry work should be done.
>
> These skills are valued by him; i.e., they are an important part of his self-concept.
>
> He feels that doing the job (for example, carrying out the decisions which he has participated in making) is in some ways a test of whether he has these skills.
>
> There is some kind of feedback which tells him whether he has passed the test.

The above analysis should help us to understand why an individ- •
ual might feel greater achievement in carrying out a decision which he made than one that he did not make. For example, if he decided to make 20 units a day, he may work harder just to prove that this is a realistic goal. If he decided to do a certain way, he may work hard just to prove that he picked the best way. Further, meeting a goal which he himself has set may be viewed as a valid test of his skills as a worker.

This analysis also suggests conditions under which participation would not lead to higher motivation. For example, participation may not work if the individuals involved do not value the skills •
tested. Thus one might predict that participation would work less well with transient day laborers than with skilled tradesmen who are proud of their craft—or with a salesman whose main interest is •
in becoming a musician than with salesmen who look upon sales as their career. Participation would also be less likely to be success- •
ful if decisions reached through participation are viewed as being trivial or as not involving a valid test of abilities.

Finally, individual participation may provide stronger motivation for achievement than does the group variety, especially if the person perceived his participative contributions as insignificant. Indeed group participation may rely less on autonomy and achieve- •
ment ("growth needs") than on the satisfaction of social needs.

2. *Group pressures:* When participation takes place in a group set-

ting, a new element is added: group pressure to conform to decisions adopted. A three-step process may be involved.

Step 1. Participation in a group discussion or decision may increase the individual's identification with or attraction to the group, particularly if he had valued the group in the first place, or if he had a high need for social approval. The mere fact of participation may make the individual feel that his status within the group had increased and thus lead to his valuing the group more highly (i.e., it now plays a more important part in his self-concept). In a sense, the individual says, "If the group wants my opinions, it must be a pretty good group; at least, since I like having my opinions considered, I better pay more attention to it."

Step 2. Once the individual values the group, he becomes more sensitive to group norms, since he wants to be a good group member. Among the group norms is that of carrying out the decisions which the group itself has made. (Normally, one would expect participation would have little impact on an assembly of individuals who have no feeling of being a group and therefore no group norms.)

Step 3. To the extent that groups (or, more exactly, individuals within groups) participate in the decisions of the larger organization, group norms may develop which support those of the larger organization (i.e., there may be greater commitment to the larger organization). If participation leads the group as a whole to feel that it has higher status within the organization, then the group may value the organization more highly and become more receptive to its norms—and enforce them. On the other hand, if these norms are not congruent with those of the larger organization, then participation in group decisions may actually render the individual less receptive to the values of the larger organization. For example, if the group promotes "bogies" or "ceilings" restricting output, then participation may result in lower production.

All this would suggest that the group participation should be highly powerful. However, for the process to work it would seem necessary for each individual to feel that he himself has made a significant contribution to the group and for the group to feel that it has significantly influenced the decisions of the organization as a whole. These conditions are often difficult to meet.

Also, participation does raise certain dangers. As group members become more involved in group processes and as cohesion increases, the group may learn to expect to be consulted about every problem which arises. Since in a large organization it may not be possible to consult everyone about every problem, expectations will often be frustrated, and perhaps it might be better not to get the members so involved.

Participation as Bargaining and Consideration

Bargaining—implicit or explicit—is a form of participation. Participation may set up an exchange relationship in which workers feel that they should work harder in return for concessions in other areas. For example, in exchange for management's agreement to let everyone go home an hour early before a big weekend, the employees may decide (with or without any explicit agreement) that they should work extra hard that day.

Participation is often a form of consideration and as such it may reduce resistance to change. As illustrated in the Scanlon Plan case discussed above, participation may make change easier, in part because it reduces resentment which may stem from the fact that orders go only one way—downward—and that workers never feel they have any say as to anything. Similarly, participation is a form of consideration in that it permits catharsis ("letting off steam") and a reduction of generalized antagonism against management or the job.

Furthermore, given the symbolic value of democracy and participation in American society, participation has become almost a form of "industrial courtesy." In many organizations there are strong expectations that the supervisor will at least "go through the motions" of eliciting participation, at least about such relatively trivial matters as how desks are to be arranged. Those who refuse to accept this convention are viewed as autocratic and nonconsiderate. The presence of limited, "mock" participation of this sort may not increase motivation or productivity; however, its absence will reduce satisfaction.

Making Participative
Management Work

The material in this chapter is based on "Improving the Quality of Work Life Managerial Practices," prepared for the U.S. Department of Labor by George Strauss, and published as PB 255 047, June 1975; and on "Participative Management and Its Role in Motivations and Productivity," by Gerald Silverman, Oklahoma University, and published as AD-A010 323, December 1974.

In order to provide creative, constructive, satisfying and productive reactions among workers, it is imperative that we learn to manage our workday affairs so as to satisfy the social and emotional needs of people. It is necessary to perceive the nature of man and his psychological problems and attempt to resolve these problems to allow him to apply his energies to creativity in work. There is a certainty that, under proper conditions, unimagined resources of creative energy could become available within the organizational setting because man is endowed with a capacity for foresight and imagination.

The structure of the organization represents a large contributing factor to the efficiency in work performance. It also contributes, to a degree, to the success of motivational programs. There have been many arguments over management methodology—the participative management system versus the classical management concept. As Bell puts it:

> Formalized structures and processes refer to the degree to which role expectations and behavior are explicitly established and regulated by the administrative apparatus. An organization is formally structured when there is extensive regulation and control of behavior. Flexible structures and processes characterize those institutions in which the majority of tasks are not gov-

erned by explicitly stated regulations and policies and in which employees are not strictly governed by rigid clearly specified authority structure.[1]

The conclusions drawn from various studies indicate clearly that the less authoritative the supervision, and the more participation by the employee in the decision role, the higher the job satisfaction indicator. This concept is in consonance with the classical psychological theory of motivation which was first advanced by A. H. Maslow. His pyramid of needs established self realization and esteem needs as the ultimate in the hierarchy.

In commenting on participative management Douglas McGregor provides us with a leveling insight to some problems by arguing that:

> Delegation is not an effective way of exercising management by control. Participation becomes a farce when it is applied as a sales gimmick or a device for kidding people into thinking they are important. Only the management that has confidence in human capacities and is itself directed toward organizational objectives rather than toward the preservation of personal power can grasp the implications of this emerging theory.[2]

It becomes evident that we must guard against canned solutions or rules, since they become highly impracticable. If participative management is pushed too far, it will become troublesome—especially where the methodology is enforced without prior planning. Dr. James Mosel states that, "If you try to give a big dose of participative management to an old-time, squads-left military organization or factory you will create havoc and probably start a revolt." The consequence would, in all probability, be randomness and uncertainty, with eventual disintegration of the organization. Conversely, should the classical management system be introduced suddenly into a "think tank" R & D environment, it too would collapse with a sudden halt to all creativity and problem solving.

WHEN TO USE PARTICIPATION

Too much writing in this field deals with participation in the abstract, rather than in terms of specific situations. And where specific situations are discussed these tend to be highly dramatic examples of radical new innovations which involve substantial departures from typical patterns of managerial behavior. Too frequently participation has been sold as a cure-all and as a consequence the concept has acquired ideological overtones. All of this serves to persuade the manager that opting for participation requires an all-or-none decision, like making a "decision for Christ." Consequently conservative managers play it safe and let others experiment with this gimmick.

However, opting for participation doesn't require an all-or-none decision. It is useful to think of participation not as something that ₄is good or bad, but as something which comes in various shades of grey. V. A. Vroom suggests that we think in terms of "feasible sets." By this he means that for every managerial problem there is a "feasible set" of alternative decision-making approaches which is generally appropriate and another set which is inappropriate. Among these forms of decision making are various varieties of participation. There are some problems for which a specific form of participation is almost absolutely required (e.g., under law management is required to "participate" with its union representatives in setting wages); there are other situations where participation is clearly counter-indicated (e.g., in many emergencies), and then there is a broad feasible set in which the degree and form of participation is largely a matter of individual managerial preference.

Conditions Affecting Participation

Thus, rather than seeking to determine the one best method of handling any given situation, managers should be encouraged to think in terms of eliminating those approaches which won't work and then to adopt from the remaining feasible set the approach which is most comfortable for them and most consistent with their own general philosophy of management. The first step, therefore, is to determine the conditions under which participation is or is not likely to succeed, i.e., the limits of the feasible set. Some of the considerations which the manager might take into account are outlined below.

Supervisory mistrust: Participation won't work—at least for long—

if the supervisor doesn't have faith in it. As M. Lufton points out, "pseudo-democratic" methods, such as nondirective listening, are quite common in such professions as social work, but are frequently used in a manipulative manner which reduces individual autonomy and leads to subordinate resentment. For participation to be successful, the supervisor should believe that the process will lead to positive results and he must be willing to accept or, at the least, give careful consideration to his subordinates' suggestions.

Supervisory trust is critical here. According to studies by Ritchie and Miles, supervisory attitudes toward their subordinates have a greater impact on subordinate job satisfaction than does the sheer amount of participatory consultancy. Where supervisors have confidence in their subordinates' abilities, satisfaction tends to be high. Where such confidence is lacking (i.e., where the supervisor views participation merely as a morale builder), the parties go through the motions of what then becomes "counterfeit participation." Employees eventually see through the deception; the desired payoff in terms of morale does not result, and productivity is even less likely to improve. Unless the supervisor trusts his subordinates, they are unlikely either to trust him or have any faith that the participatory process affords them any influence. Only when trust is present are subordinates likely to express their views with honesty.

The fact that a supervisor has a participative attitude or philosophy does not mean that he is required to hold endless meetings, to consult at length prior to taking action during emergencies, or to discuss endless trivia. Indeed, subordinates will generally mistrust participatory gestures if they are inconsistent with the supervisor's overall leadership style and may well perceive them as a form of manipulation rather than genuine power sharing.

Personality and culture: Individual personality factors are certainly relevant. Research suggests that those with authoritarian personalities and low need for independence are likely to react relatively unfavorably to participation. Similarly, it would seem likely that high need achievement would have to be present were participation to operate via providing a sense of achievement—and high need affiliation would have to be present were it to operate via group pressures.

Cultural and occupational factors are also important. There may be substantial differences between cultures in terms of the value given to participation or willingness to accept the responsibility for making suggestions, particularly in the presence of the boss (especially if he is viewed himself as representing another culture). For example, workers in some countries such as India feel decision making is top management's job, not that of the workers. There are also differences among occupational groups. Professionals tend to value participation more than nonprofessionals, and in collegiate organizations, such as many universities, nonparticipative activities fall outside the feasible set.

Organizational commitment: As Douglas McGregor put it, "Theory Y assumes that people will exercise self-direction and self-control in the achievement of organizational objectives *to the degree that they are committed to these objectives.*"[2] On the other hand, participation is a means of generating such commitment. (E.g., the best way to get a charitable gift is to put rich donors on the fund-raising committee.)

Subordinates are at least unconsciously aware that the price they pay for participation is commitment; and for some, this price is too high. To the extent that people resist commitment they will also reject participation. Apparently there are large subcultures of employees who view participation as reducing their freedom. P. M. Blau's study of civil servants suggests that "the group's insistence that the supervisor discharge his duty issuing directives—that's what he gets paid for— serves to emphasize that their obedience to him does not constitute submission to his will but adherence, on his part as well as theirs, to abstract principles which they have socially accepted."[3] And among these principles is limited commitment to organizational objectives.

Organizational atmosphere: The success of participation in a given situation depends heavily on the atmosphere in the organization as a whole. Participation will be less likely to be successful where there has been a history of labor-management strife or if management at all levels has been autocratic in the past. If the organization is generally authoritarian, attempts to bootleg participation into a single department or work group face difficulties unless the rest of the organization is involved and/or appropriate adjustment made.

Organizational structure may also discourage participation. If the supervisor has little discretion, he has little opportunity to implement subordinate suggestions. The more centralized and more rulebound the organization, the less opportunity there is for subordinates to develop new ways of doing things.

Nature of the decision-making task: There are certain subjects which are appropriate for only fairly restricted forms of participation. Given company legal obligations, the question of whether to desegregate a department is probably not appropriate for participation; the question of how to do it is. Fruitful participation is not likely to occur over the question of whether a company should make layoffs during a recession; nevertheless, the company should be prepared to consider suggestions for alternative means to save money and allow fairly full participation in determining how to implement such a layoff unless this question has already been determined through union negotiations.

Actually, there are many areas in which management does not care what decision is made, so long as there is no excessive dissension. For example, management is unconcerned with how men divide up the dirty work as long as the work is done—or how rest periods are divided up, so long as the time allotted is not exceeded. Since no vacation schedule can satisfy everyone, the manager who can pass the scheduling responsibility to the group saves himself a major headache. (Note, however, that the supervisor still must preside over the process by which the decision is made. If he says merely "You decide" without helping to establish a procedure by which the decision can be made, there may be endless bickering and confusion. It is the supervisor's responsibility to help the group resolve its internal difficulties.)

In other areas the supervisor's objectives coincide with those of the group—in matters of accident-prevention or avoiding jam-ups in the parking lot, for example. Possibly management should reserve a veto power over decisions in such matters, although it is unlikely that the group will make decisions that are, from the supervisor's point of view, far wrong.

The supervisor, of course, is interested not only in getting a sound decision, but also one that is accepted by the group. An adequate decision that is enthusiastically implemented may well be better than a perfect solution that meets with stubborn antagonism. Thus the participative process is particularly appropriate where the supervisor is concerned more with getting acceptance of a decision than with its quality.

However, there are a number of other areas which are probably not appropriate for participation. A crisis demanding immediate decisions is not the time to call a formal meeting. On the other hand, such a meeting may be useful, if held before the crisis, to develop procedures in advance of need. Furthermore, a participative atmosphere and experience in working together to develop plans will result in greater teamwork when the crisis actually occurs.

Inappropriate subjects for participation may also be those about which subordinates have little information, few requisite skills, and/or little concern for the final results. Even so, the assignment of such "novel" problems to a work group may widen its members' horizons, develop their personal skills, and pherhaps generate fresh new thoughts unsullied by conventional wisdom.

LIMITATIONS AND PAYOFFS

Ideally, the supervisor provides broad areas of freedom in which subordinates can regulate their own behavior (this is simply teamwork). However, there are bound to be areas of basic conflict between superiors and subordinates—i.e., at one time or another, every boss must face the inevitability of making and announcing distasteful decisions. The question thus arises of how a supervisor can keep a meeting from encroaching on areas of decision making that are not its proper concern.

One way of dealing with such issues is to set clear *limits* to the group's area of freedom. For example, instead of asking his subordinates "How much vacation time should you get?", the supervisor might ask "How many people can we spare at any one time during vacation and still meet customer needs?"—i.e., "Who should go when?" And he should make it clear in advance that he reserves the right to reject proposed group decisions if he feels that (from his point of view) their "quality" falls below an acceptable minimum. Then the most he can do is explain why he has rejected a particular decision and perhaps ask for questions.

Rewards for participation: As much of the foregoing suggests, for participation to be more than "counterfeit" and for employees to be enthusiastic, it needs to provide significant payoffs (valued rewards) to all those involved. One payoff is increased influence for everyone. But workers may feel that intangible rewards, such as the sheer pleasure of additional responsibility, is not reward enough; they may also want higher pay. One of the strengths of the Scanlon Plan is that the higher production resulting from participation gets rewarded in solid cash.

Cognitive dissonance and equity enter here. When workers work harder or more efficiently, they see the company making more money, and they want more pay themselves. Thus, when workers take on managerial tasks, it should not be surprising if they seek some (tangible) compensation for themselves.

Possible Payoffs

There are a variety of possible payoffs from participation. Much of the discussion, here and elsewhere, has emphasized direct productivity, which may be among the hardest of payoffs to obtain, among other reasons because productivity is a function of many things besides supervisory behavior and subordinate motivation. Among the other and more likely rewards from participation are greater group cohesion, reduction of resistance to change, better communications, reduced alienation, and improved job satisfaction (especially when subordinates are strong in need achievement or need affiliation and when the concept of participation is accepted as legitimate in the local culture).

One especially important payoff, commonly ignored, is the better organization of work. Indeed, participation is often thought of as a motivator (and has been so treated here). In practice it may play an even more important role as a form of consideration and work facilitation. Another significant payoff is increased managerial power in the sense that participation increases rather than decreases the boss's influence. The boss may gain a better feel for what his subordinates are thinking, he obtains the benefit of their suggestions, and, above all, he has some commitment from them to implement agreed upon plans. Thus the organization, management, and employees alike can all benefit from valued, relevant forms and degrees of participation.

Questions and Answers
on Quality of Worklife Programs

The material in this chapter is based on "Improving the Quality of Worklife . . . and in the Process, Improving Productivity," prepared for the Manpower Administration, U.S. Department of Labor, by Edward M. Glaser, Human Interaction Institute, and published as PB 236 209, August 1974.

The following are some questions frequently raised concerning company efforts to embark on the quality of worklife and productivity improvement programs.

1. Is every company capable of undertaking a quality of work program?

No. The top management and the supporting cast have to "give a damn"—even if they do it only to reduce labor problems and increase profits. Beyond a willing spirit, there must also be the patience and readiness to sustain a deep commitment. If a quality of work activity is not painstakingly planned, based upon careful diagnosis of problems and an assessment of learning readiness, it probably will fail.

2. If a company seems incapable of undertaking what might be termed a humanization of work program, what changes are needed to gain such capability?

This depends on the reasons for the company's unwillingness, inability or non-readiness. In some cases management and/or union attitudes and practices need attention first. In other cases, the main obstacle may be in the technology, or a negligible labor involvement in a highly automated production process, or be based upon certain fears of losing control or of "stirring up the natives," or concerns about the reward system that might need to be revamped.

How enterprises can best make the necessary changes depends

first on finding leadership that wants to explore the new directions. Next comes personal contact with similar companies who are using such plans; and the finding of competent technical assistance for a study of their situation. This is followed by collaborative planning by all people necessary for successful implementation, and a pilot tryout.

Qualified consultants may be able to help in the role of resource persons, catalysts, facilitators of learning readiness, and trainers when/if readiness is present.

3. Have worklife improvement programs to date been limited to small companies in the Western world using mainly middle-class employees?

No. Large companies in both Japan and India, as well as large and small companies in the U.S. and in Europe, have tested and are still experimenting with ways to improve the quality of work and increase productivity. Many U.S. companies are doing so with a work force classified as disadvantaged.

It is interesting to note here, however, that most of the very large corporations reporting noteworthy success with job enrichment or efforts to improve the quality of worklife in some division of their company (AT&T, General Electric, General Foods, Imperial Chemical, Motorola, Procter and Gamble) have not as yet introduced these successful programs throughout the firm, whereas some smaller companies like Donnelly Mirrors have carried the principles into all segments of their operation.

4. Is there any evidence that good results from the experimental programs are sustained?

Yes, but not always. Few cases reported in the literature evaluate change over time, but there are several longitudinal studies. Some companies have been operating cost-savings sharing or productivity sharing plans, which include worker participation in job design, for up to 35 years with continued good results as measured by reduction in labor costs, in grievances, in turnover, in absenteeism and in machine downtime—all parts of increased general productivity. Other companies not using group financial incentives (AT&T, Motorola, Polaroid, Procter and Gamble, Texas Instruments) have achieved and sustained desirable results from job enrichment efforts for lengths of time varying from three to eight or nine years.

5. Do we assume that most workers today are alienated, or that most workers would respond favorably to a job enrichment program?

Based upon the available survey evidence, most workers do not now feel alienated. But, in many situations, most workers do evince some degree of alienation. An overall approach to the humanization of work seems to be desired by most, but not all workers, according to reports from companies with well-planned programs of employee involvement in job design and other matters which affect them. Those who do not want increased responsibility or do not want to learn new skills will need a specially tailored approach to cope with their feelings. This minority should be permitted to continue in their still-needed and familiar tasks so long as they perform satisfactorily. As Sam Zagoria, director of the Labor-Management Relations Service of the National League of Cities has observed, "All workers are not alike; they are not cast from the same mold. They come in assorted shapes, sizes, education and experience, attitudes and ambitions. Some work for a living; for others working is living. Some think of work as their central purpose in life; others consider work as a way of providing the necessities and look to the time away from work as the real joy of living. The net of this is that while many workers look on their jobs as unexciting, boring, repetitive exercises that require only part of their potential capability, others enjoy the regularity, repetiton, and steadiness of a job. They are delighted to leave to management all the headaches and heartaches of a competitive, high risk economy. Truly, one man's straitjacket may be another's security blanket. . . ." In sum, workers vary in their job objectives. For most, whether by conscious choice or unconscious acceptance of life as they find it, a job which provides a living is enough. For others, and it suspected they are increasing in number, taking home a paycheck is not enough—they want a chance for self-fulfillment in the many years they spend in the workplace.

6. We read a lot about firms such as AT&T, Donnelly Mirrors, General Foods, Motorola, Polaroid, Texas Instruments, where efforts to improve organizational effectiveness and efficiency through quality of work programs have been successful. Have there been many failures or disappointments following such efforts?

Yes. Indeed there have been failures and disappointments. To borrow a concept from the psychology of learning, quality of work programs do not present a simple Stimulus → Response situation. If you apply a hot flame (stimulus) to any normal person's skin, you will get an "ouch"—or pain response. Instead, the learning principle here can be diagrammed: S → C → O → R. S, the stimulus (quality of work program) is applied under C, certain conditions, including given qualities of appropriate planning, skill and timing to O, an organization having its own history, readiness for change, feelings of commitment (or lack thereof) . . . all of which then lead to R, certain responses and results.

In other words, the same fire can melt the butter or harden the egg. Nevertheless it would seem that when a program has been successful in many organizations with different sorts of people and under different conditions there is something to generalize about the principles involved. The fact remains, however, that in a number of cases, job enrichment efforts have not worked out well and have been discontinued. There may be things which can be generalized from those experiences too. Perhaps the question regarding failure experiences might be compared with a medical or surgical procedure—which, although helpful in many cases, has not worked out well in others. It may be in the variables: the condition of the patient at the time of treatment, the diagnosis, the appropriateness of the intervention, the skill of the physician, the degree of intelligent cooperation of the patient, the treatment and care in preparation for as well as following the surgery, etc.

7. If the favorable results reported from a number of the quality of worklife improvement programs have some generalizable characteristics, what are they? Are there dimensions of the person-organization-environment interactions that seem essential to successful outcomes in diverse settings?

Yes, to a degree, but not with certainty. Some of the dimensions that make a difference seem to be: (1) sustained commitment from management to the open, non-defensive modus operandi of sincerely inviting collaborative inputs from the work force regarding problem identification and suggestions for improving any aspect of the organization or the policies, practices and structure of work, with incentives provided for such participation; (2) invited involvement of members of task groups in recommending resolution of identified problems; (3) training of supervisors to equip them to function effectively in this less directive style; (4) implementation of practicable suggestions and explanations for rejected ideas; (5) feedback, and recognition for good results achieved; (6) selection of personnel who can be motivated, under appropriate conditions, to "give a damn" about striving for excellence in task performance; (7) evaluation and analysis of results, including failures, leading to revised efforts toward continual improvement in modus operandi.

8. Why, in spite of clear evidence of significant gains in productivity following the establishment of job enrichment programs in given companies, has there been no follow-through? In some cases, the program has been scuttled, when compelling evidence points to success. Why?

Some partial answers can be given. These programs can pose a psychological threat to some managers, union leaders, and the bureaucracy. The concept of inviting workers to have voice and influence in all aspects of a task, the setting up of autonomous work teams, and the providing of open channels of communication at all levels does mean giving up some of the conventional authority exercised by the company—or union—bosses. With dubious commitment at the start, relatively minor problems or costs can be readily exaggerated, followed by reversion to traditional, more comfortable ways of operating. Further, in some cases the initial good results in fact do not continue—for a variety of reasons in particular situations, such as loss of initial internal leadership, commitment and skills; new technical problems; unforeseen stress and crisis; equity issues; collective bargaining dynamics; etc.

9. Why have so few companies tried upgrading the quality of life at work when the evidence of promising results and the description of methodology frequently have appeared in the management, personnel and behavioral science literature since the early 1960s?

Again, there are only opinions on this unanswered but important question. As above, it involves management's fear of losing control or attenuating management prerogatives, responsibility and authority by inviting participation in decision making from persons "down the line" (and perhaps their union representatives). At the same time it may evoke a union's fear of losing status with its members if an individual worker's ideas and suggestions can be discussed directly with a receptive management in a "non-adversary" climate. Further, job enrichment efforts require a willingness (and time-patience) to engage in considerable planning *with* the work force before making decisions which affect them. Many organizations feel uncomfortable with this style of management. In addition, if the work force below them in the hierarchy is invited to identify the things that need improvement, some managers (consciously or unconsciously) fear *their* boss may wonder why they seemingly hadn't been aware of those problems or needs/opportunities for improvement, and thus perhaps wonder about their capability or whether they are "on top of things."

Solid research evidence, however, still is lacking for a well-documented answer to this question.

10. If you asked all personnel in organizations reporting success with their quality of work programs if they would continue to organize and structure the work the way it is now, or change it, what would the probable answer be?

Continue, but with continual review and openness to refinement based upon experience. In the few situations where this questioning has been tried, informal results report some 80% of the personnel expressed a desire to continue the consultative format.

Case Histories

The material in this chapter is based on "Improving the Quality of Worklife...and in the Process, Improving Productivity," prepared for the Manpower Administration, U.S. Department of Labor, by Edward M. Glaser, Human Interaction Institute, and published as PB 236 209, August 1974.

The case histories selected here deal with a broad spectrum of situations. Some of the principles involved in quality of worklife improvement, such as inviting the work force to participate or become ego-involved in problem or opportunity identification and problem solving, are common to all situations. In other cases the restructuring and reorganization of work seems a key ingredient. In some instances the program seemed highly successful for a few years, then faltered badly when top management changed and the needed commitment was no longer present.

MEDICAL SPECIALTIES COMPANY

This case illustrates, among other things, what can be accomplished when a company announces that part of its operation must become profitable or be discontinued. The program started with the top man in a given department inviting his subordinates to participate in problem identification and problem solving.

By way of background information it may be said that Medical Specialties Company manufactures and distributes some 800 products and has an annual sales volume of over $80 million. The top management structure is conventional: a president who is also chief executive officer, an executive vice president, and vice presidents for marketing, manufacturing, finance and research. There are also some wholly-owned subsidiaries, each with its own president. Management can be described as conservative, somewhat paternalistic and interested in sound development and expansion. The company prides itself in being fair and considerate of its employees.

In 1965, the vice president in charge of manufacturing called in one of the psychologists who had been consulting with the company since 1950, to work with a department that had been losing money steadily on an item produced in twenty variations. Low productivity, too many labor grievances and high operating costs were among his concerns. The consultant first met with the department head, who had his own bones of contention: the sales department turned in too many small orders on the varieties of the product; the engineering department demanded tolerance standards that were too close for economical mass production; the suppliers delivered poor raw materials, and so on. When the consultant then talked to the heads of the sales, engineering and quality control departments, each passed the buck back to the others involved.

Psychological objective number one was to change the name of the game—and the reward system—from survival by taking no blame, to frankly admitting problems and solving them—or perish.

The consultant, with the concurrence of the manufacturing vice president, suggested that the president decide what percentage of his market his company could reasonably expect to capture if design, price, quality and service were first-rate. After establishing this estimate, the president advised the appropriate people in maufacturing-engineering-sales that unless they could come up with a sure-fire plan to capture the agreed-on share of the market, the company would discontinue that set of products, and lay off some sixty hourly rate workers.

This ultimatum from the president *supplied a very powerful motivating force.* Those concerned met and decided that they did not want to go out of business. In short order, a number of plans were evolved. Among them: the redesign of the product set and the addition of a technical service man in each region to help the users with any problems they might have.

Implementing the new plans, however, would cost considerable money. The president agreed to provide the additional funds only if those who recommended the plan guaranteed it would bring the desired results. Their necks were on the line, so to speak, and so, with some gulping, they agreed to the plan. With the ultimatum in force, those concerned were glad to have a consultant available to them.

The consultant first made a psychological evaluation of the manufacturing department head and his two male supervisors. This evaluation report, designed to enhance personal insight development, was then fed back to each man in a private counseling session. When the consultant felt that the leadership in the department was sufficiently nondefensive, the department head invited the five female sub-supervisors—union members as well as a part of management—for a meeting with him and his two male supervisors.

The union was consulted and, after it expressed no objection, the consultant, the department head and these seven supervisory personnel joined in a frank and honest attempt to define problems, opportunities, goals and means of goal-attainment. The department manager set the climate nicely. He explained the consultant's role as a resource person on hand to facilitate problem solving and communication among these members of the departmental group. He then stated that the first person to identify the manager as the key problem would win a lace umbrella or some other suitable reward.

The manager further reassured those present that any increase in productivity or improvement in quality to result from their problem-solving would be translated into efforts to expand sales. Management had already agreed that no worker would be laid off, no matter how great an increase in productivity might be achieved.

In the next thirty-five minutes, twenty-eight work problems were identified and organized under appropriate headings. Two of the suggestions for change were simple enough to implement (e.g., protection for the workers against a hot afternoon sun coming into the windows of their work station). The department head said "yes" to these immediately. Two other proposed changes he knew could not be brought about (one would have constituted a violation of the state labor law). To these he said "no" immediately, giving clear and persuasive reasons.

The remaining twenty-four suggestions needed further investigation of some sort: fact finding, cost analysis, feasibility study, cooperation of other departments, or authorization from a higher level. Ad hoc volunteer committees were formed to look into those suggestions for which implementation authority resided in the department, and report their recommended action plan.

Within three months every suggestion was answered with either: "We'll do it," or "Analysis reveals that it isn't feasible for the following reasons," or "We can do it in part, or in modified form." At the end of the same three-month period, productivity was up 32%, rejects had dropped from 12% to 9%, and there had not been a single labor grievance. Feedback of any progress on productivity, reduction of labor grievances, machine downtime, absenteeism, turnover and rejects was supplied periodically to the entire group.

The supervisors came to realize that under the new system positive reinforcement would be given for openly admitting and solving problems. They held relaxed post-mortem reviews of the department's results, asking themselves and each other, "How can we do it better?" Communication became freer and more honest. The entire group felt the new spirit of action. They were actively participating in the goals of the department and in the organization of the work to achieve those goals. A sense of responsibility for their own destiny developed. Now there was an opportunity to try out creative innovations and encouragement to become ego-involved.

These supervisors, then, became industrially active people—rather than industrially reactive. As a result of their suggestions, work was restructured and jobs enriched. They found new meaning in mass-producing products—the same products which had previously been produced with such travail. They found greater pleasure in their work now—and chose to invest more of themselves in trying to increase productivity and find greater job satisfaction for all involved.

After the first three months, the sixty-plus hourly employees were invited to participate. At the first meeting they were divided into subgroups of twelve. These subgroups came up with seventy-eight ideas. Again, some suggestions were settled on the spot. Others required study, and the employees were invited to volunteer for ad hoc committees to conduct such study and recommend appropriate action. The majority did so volunteer; no pressure was exerted to get anyone to volunteer who did not spontaneously do so.

In the following weeks and months, many of the employee ideas were adopted, in whole or in part. Improvements were made in product design, work structure and departmental organization, as well as in what might be classified "comfort" items or working conditions. Periodic reports were made to the hourly workers, either in department meetings or in writing. The people were shown that their efforts were not only appreciated but acted on by management. Ego-boundaries were enlarged. There were satisfactions from cooperative achievement. The employees truly were participating—if they volunteered to do so—in the activities and decisions that affected them. No one needed to file a formal grievance to be heard open-mindedly on any subject he might wish to bring up. And, while there was no guarantee that their ideas would find agreement, the implicit guarantee was that they would be treated with dignity and respect, and given explanations on why any suggestions were not adopted.

The results of the experiment were impressive:

1. Labor grievances dropped from an average of one a week in 1965 to only one grievance in three years (1966-1968).

2. Three months after the intervention, production rose 32% and the reject rate fell from 12% to 9%. Then, following the intervention of all members of the department, productivity continued to climb. In 1968 it was an almost unbelievable 190% greater than the 1965 baseline, while rejects dropped to 3.2%.

3. Average labor turnover and absenteeism dropped significantly.

4. Improvement continued *under the group's own motivation* through repeated application of the principles and procedures initially used in this program. The consultant tapered off his aid after one year. The group, under the able leadership of the department head, continued to achieve fine results.

5. Department operations had increased substantially in both complexity and volume during this 1965-1969 period of time, and have continued to increase since then.

It should be emphasized that if any employee did not find the more responsible involvement in the work personally satisfying, no pressure was exerted to persuade that individual to do more. The employee could then leave the problem solving and decision making to others, as long as his own performance was reasonably satisfactory. Thus, individual differences with regard to desire for participative involvement were respected.

And most important to note, all of the improvements reported above came from the people in the department, including departmental management and supervision, supported by engineering staff help on some items, or product engineering assistance, or feedback from the sales department regarding customer acceptance or complaints. All the consultant did was to help develop a nondefensive climate which permitted constructive and creative challenge of standard practice, a climate and some skills (such as listening skills) which facilitated problem identification, problem solving, and the implementation of progressive change.

Comment: The fact that the remarkable substantive improvement noted in the experiment with the single department did not get picked up for deliberate cross-validation trial in other parts of the company illustrates not only the key importance of sustained internal advocacy and powerful support for an innovation of this kind, without which it is likely to wither for lack of reinforcing nourishment, but it also suggests that such commitment was lacking at certain key levels.

Probably another and more subtle reason for the fact that the experiment cited did not spread within the plant is that part of the support that was voiced came from the president of the company during that time period (this president died prematurely a few years thereafter). In his enthusiasm as an observer, and perhaps partly because of a very cordial relationship with the consultant, he suggested that other departments in the plant might well try that kind of consulting help. This tended to give the impression that he felt the consultant was primarily responsible for the gains achieved, whereas in fact all the substantive ideas were developed by the people themselves, some of whom literally worked day and night to refine and implement the suggestions which were generated. What was perceived as over-credit to the consultant led to displeasure and resistance from others who very understandably felt that they should have received by far the major recognition.

Problems of the sort noted above can influence the viability and vitality of the exciting experiment in a new plant. At least there is awareness of them. To date, the new plant start-up is coming along well, supported (1) by an enthusiastic plant manager and his staff; (2) by some persons at the corporate office headquarters; (3) by a research and demonstration project grant from the U.S. Department of Labor to permit planning and start-up consultation to help this new plant organize and structure the operation along job enrichment lines; (4) by another Department of Labor grant to an independent evaluation team from a major university to see what can be learned and verified for possible generalization to other work situations. When the outside supports are withdrawn, however, it is predicted that unless a deeper, more powerful and more sustained commitment can be developed at the corporate level to the objective appraisal of the net-balance value of this more demanding style of management, it will not spread within the corporation. At best, the particular plant that has this interest and dedication will be allowed to proceed in its own way, so long as the results seem clearly good, and so long as the plant manager firmly retains his commitment to that type of modus operandi.

DONNELLY MIRRORS INC., HOLLAND, MICHIGAN

A relatively small (600 employees), family-owned company, Donnelly supplies nearly 70% of all automotive mirrors used in the United States.

For twenty years Donnelly has used a modified version of the Scanlon Plan of cost-savings sharing. In that same time, the company has had a compounded growth rate of 14% and return on investment has tripled. According to President John F. Donnelly, the corporation competes successfully with other companies in the community in basic wages, and also pays bonuses which, over the past decade, have averaged 10% a month.

In 1967, Donnelly added yet another participative management program. With the help of behavioral scientists from the University of Michigan, the company organized all of its employees into small work teams. The teams, according to a Donnelly report:

> Have a common responsibility for part of the organization's work. . .made up of a supervisor or manager and the subordinates who report to him. . .an effective team is normally composed of a maximum of fifteen or twenty people, and should not be so large as to be cumbersome. Work team meetings are usually held once a month or oftener if an emergency situation arises. . . . The purpose and function of the work team is to set goals and develop plans for their team, to determine how best to carry out their work and to solve their own problems and make their own decisions whenever possible. We have found that teams are capable of making good economic decisions.

Among the specific responsibilities taken over by the work teams are participating in interviewing and hiring new team members, handling disciplinary problems, and helping to select new supervisors. Central to the Donnelly concept of participative management is the presence of the "linking pin":

> The linking pin means that the manager or supervisor of each work team is also a member of the next highest group. It is his membership in this higher team that links (integrates) his team with the rest of the organization. As a manager works with his peers in the planning process or decision making, he may hold a decision in abeyance, should he feel the need for more input from the team he is responsible for. . . . It is not uncommon for a management team. . .or for any work team to call in members from other teams to get better and first hand information before making a decision. The interlocking team structure and group process described, with the link pin functioning as described, allows an amazing flow of ideas. It further insures that no single person or group can force their ideas on others, and it eliminates a great deal of misinformation and rumor.

In 1970 all Donnelly employees who formerly had been paid on an hourly basis were put on salary. All time clocks were removed. Under the new policy, pressure for good performance comes from other team members rather than from superiors. Work teams also have no reservations about reducing the number of jobs, since workers profit from increased productivity. Employees who are eliminated from their jobs in the interests of improved efficiency are assured work elsewhere in the company. And, as production costs are reduced by job eliminations, bonuses go up.

Donnelly work teams are encouraged to contribute suggestions. One maintenance man developed a machine for $290 that would have cost the company $900 to buy. In another instance, the production worker who was to operate a new piece of equipment was among those sent to California to test and give his approval before purchase.

Annual pay increases at Donnelly are established by a committee in which employees participate. In one recent year, workers asked for increases totaling $292,000. The corporation agreed, providing the employees could come up with suggestions for equal cost reductions.

In twenty years Donnelly estimates that productivity per person has doubled. In the past five years, quality control personnel has dropped from fourteen to four. Other positive signs: a marked reduction in returned goods, absenteeism down from 5% to 1½ %, tardiness from 6% to less than 1%, and a worker turnover so small it is not worth recording. Donnelly credits the last three improvements to the end-of-the-time-clock program.

Senior Vice President, Richard N. Arthur, described the Donnelly experience at the "Changing Work Ethic" conference in New York in March 1973. "We believe that every person is creative and wants to make a contribution," he concluded. "From that, we see it as our responsibiliy to tap the creativity and contributions of our people. We can, by our way of managing, either have their creativity on our side or against us."

Comment: Donnelly Mirrors is one of the most successful examples of a long-term (20-year) commitment to improving the quality of worklife in the U.S. It must be remembered, of course, that Donnelly is a relatively small firm and a nonunion shop, both factors which allow management more flexibiliy in introducing new ideas. Still, Donnelly's record is impressive. Small work teams play an active and far-reaching role in the company, participating in everything from goal-setting to the selection of new supervisors. This degree of privilege and responsibility given to a non-supervisory work force is rare.

GAINES PET FOOD PLANT, TOPEKA, KANSAS

In this case, the Tavistock socio-technical system concept was used to plan, staff, and organize a small new plant. Gaines Pet Food is part of the Post Division of General Foods. Like Donnelly Mirrors, General Foods extended to employees such privileges and responsibilities as recruiting, hiring, disciplining, firing—normally considered supervisory functions.

The following report is summarized from a paper by Lyman D. Ketchum, General Foods manager of Organization-Operations, and was presented at the American Association for the Advancement of Science symposium, "Humanizing of Work," in Philadelphia, Pennsylvania in December 1972.

In February 1971, General Foods opened a new dog food plant in Topeka with a new work approach. According to management: "Humans will best respond (be productive) when there exists a high feeling of self-worth by the employee, and employee identification with success of the total organization."

The new plant was planned to minimize a static hierarchy of job classifications, abolish lockstep work assignments, and give all employees a voice in the running of the plant. It took two years of planning to put the plant into operation. A four-man primary project team (including the leader who would become plant manager and an engineer) began with a statement of its principles:

1. People have ego needs. They want self-esteem, a sense of accomplishment, autonomy, increasing knowledge and skill, data on their performance. People invest more in situations that allow them to meet these needs.

2. An individual has a need to be able to see himself as a significant part of the whole—be it his position in a human group or his role in a complex technology.

3. People have social needs. They enjoy team membership and teamwork. At the same time, they enjoy friendly rivalry.

4. People want to be able to identify with products they produce and firms that employ them. People care especially about the quality of things with which they can identify.

5. People have certain security needs. They want reasonable income and employment security, and want to be assured against arbitrary and unfair treatment. They also want to be assured of due process.

To staff the new plant, the following advertisement was run in Topeka and Kansas City newspapers:

GENERAL FOODS NEEDS PRODUCTION SUPERVISORS

to take on a new plant and an exciting new management concept in Topeka, Kansas.

General Foods, a leading processor and distributor of nationally advertised grocery products including such household names as Post cereals, Kool-Aid, Maxwell House coffee, and many others, is opening a new Post Division plant. In the General Foods' tradition of progressive, forward-thinking management, a young new-breed idea in management is being introduced in the new facility.

If you're looking for something different, a flexible management structure that emphasizes individual abilities, an imaginative program that will set the pace for our multi-billion dollar industry, you may be the young-thinking leader we need.

You must have mechanical skill-potential with a background in production. Previous supervisory experience desirable. You will need an above-average flair for working with people and ideas—with the very minimum of supervision. Excellent salary, benefits, and relocation pay.

Thirty candidates applied for the jobs, and interviews eliminated twenty of these. The project team, advised by a consultant, then offered a weekend of problem solving, exercise and game play designed to show the attributes an individual would need to be a team leader. Six of the ten candidates were then chosen. One of the four rejected became a foreman in the parent plant, two requested jobs as team members—and one of these was hired.

The next step, according to Ketchum, was to help the new supervisors develop interpersonal skills and a knowledge of group dynamics consistent with the value system:

> It was important that the team leaders' worklife from the very beginning should be consistent with this system. Other skill development: technology, where the parent plant was used; business methods such as cost accounting, quality control, personnel procedures, capital programs, profit planning and so forth.

> One important task this new group performed was job design. With the system characteristics as given, our agreed-upon notions of people needs, knowledge of the process and opportunity to observe a similar process in the parent plant, the jobs were designed. Then began more specific work on the compensation system.

> With the plant still under construction and start-up approaching, there was a need for team members. Another transition in primary responsibility and control occurred at this phase.

> The direct role of the three primary project team members began to diminish. The team leaders began exercising more autonomy in the process of recruiting and selecting, just as the project team without the plant manager had done earlier in their recruiting and selection. This again was consistent with the value system, and was made even more practical by the knowledge and experience the team leaders had gained in their own recruitment and selection process aided by their having strongly "bought in" to the new value system. They thus, with outside help, established the criteria, designed advertising, worked out testing and selection processes and, indeed, did their own hiring.

A newspaper want ad was again used to find workers:

GENERAL FOODS TOPEKA PLANT NEEDS
PRODUCTION PEOPLE

Work in a new, modern Gaines Pet Food plant with an exciting new organization concept which will allow you to participate in all phases of plant operations.

Qualifications:

- Mechanical aptitude
- Willing to accept greater responsibility
- Willing to work rotating shifts
- Desire to learn multiple jobs and new skills

Of the 625 people who applied, all but 98 were eliminated by various screening methods. The team leaders again designed a selection weekend that eliminated an additional 35, leaving 63 who were offered jobs.

> Anyone rejected was offered...the reasons for rejection. We felt this was only right with regard to the applicant and, also, it provided the team leader an early opportunity to deal openly and honestly with people.

> It is our opinion that the team member selection process, managed in large part by the team leaders with outside consultant help, was a better process than the first designed process for selection of team leaders. This was one of our earliest reinforcements that we were on the right track in having high expectations of people when we provided them the resources and the opportunity to work on their own.

> Systematic orientation and training then took place. Committees for safety, disaster and fire protection, recreation, and so forth, were formed.

> The start-up, while not without problems, has gone satisfactorily. Learning is taking place at higher than ex-

pected rates. The plant is manned with about two-thirds the number we would expect with traditional methods.

We have learned a lot. We are still learning. Our Board of Directors has just authorized a second plant for this site. All of the learning from our first experience will be incorporated into the second. We have the opportunity in the second plant to introduce the requirements of the social system to the physical design process at the preliminary engineering phase. We will thus jointly optimize the social and technical systems, an opportunity we partially missed in the first plant.

Highlights of the Topeka program include:

Building production around team units rather than the individual worker. The three components at Topeka are teams for: (1) processing, (2) packing and shipping, (3) office duties. Each worker is assigned to a team, but not to a fixed task within the team. Rather, the total team is given the assignment, and the workers who make up the team can rotate jobs. This is proving to increase worker versatility, stimulate continuing learning, and—of primary importance—relieve boredom and the sense of doing meaningless work.

Allocating a team leader to each team—someone who is not a foreman, supervisor, watchdog or boss, but, more accurately, a coach and resource person.

Arriving at team decisions after open discussion. Among the matters subject to team decision are: individual job assignments, including how to fill in for an absent member; interviewing and hiring job applicants; establishing and changing work rules, operating decisions and policies; evaluation of individual job performance to determine need for improvement; progression within the compensation system.

Encouraging initiative. To cite an example, there are no separate maintenance or utility departments in the plant. If there is an emergency in processing or in the packing lines, it is handled by the person within a team who has the necessary skills for that specific task. While he is dealing with the emergency, his position is covered by other team members.

Assigning two production teams to handle quality control. This means that the worker who makes the product
passes judgment on its suitability; the result is a sense of
having a personal stake in doing satisfactory work.

Eliminating many of the physical manifestations of status. The office of the Operations Manager is completely
open to view and any employee can get in to see him
readily. The conference room is open to all personnel.
All employees enter and leave by the same doors. There
is no time clock. There are no reserved postions in the
parking lot. The carpeting in the manager's office is the
same as the carpeting in the locker room of the production workers.

Management has reported a discernible improvement in employee morale and in the entire work climate. There is improved
job satisfaction, more sense of responsibility and an increased
level of cooperation reported in comparison with the company's
other pet food plant in Kankakee, Illinois.

A spin-off of the job enrichment program at the Topeka plant has
been an increase in safety. The heart of the program is the safety
committee, composed of eleven people—three from each shift,
one from the office staff, and the plant safety coordinator. All
members are volunteers and meet every two weeks, usually from
one to three hours. Members carry the results of committee decisions back to their teams. According to the Bureau of Labor Statis-
tics (all work-related injuries and illnesses are considered), in 1973
the Topeka plant had 4.4 injuries and illnesses per 100 full-time
workers. The comparable rate for the food products industry as a
whole is 19.3, and for all General Foods plants in the United States
it is 7.2. There have been only two lost-time accidents in the
plant's history.

Professor Richard E. Walton of the Harvard Business School has
served as a consultant to General Foods at the Topeka plant. Since
his thinking underlies the development of the work setup, Walton's observations regarding problems encountered are important. The following summary of his main points has been taken
from his article entitled, "How to Counter Alienation in the Plant"
in the November-December 1972 issue of *Harvard Business Review*.

A major problem cited by Professor Walton was the matter of compensation. There are four basic pay rates: starting rate, single job rate for mastering the first assignment, team rate for mastering all jobs within the team's jurisdiction, and plant rate. Virtually all employees in the initial work force were hired at the same time, and at the end of the first six weeks most of them had qualified for their single job rate. Five months later, however, about one-third of the members of each team had been awarded the team rate. The decisions concerning individual pay had for the the most part been made by team leaders, and the entire issue was discussed openly, with operators participating. Despite this openness, there remained questions concerning the fairness of the evaluation made concerning the compensation awarded the individual operator.

Another source of difficulty stemmed from the reluctance and general uneasiness on the part of management, which displayed a traditional resistance to innovation. In the opinion of Professor Walton, it was paramount that this be overcome since in his judgment involvement of the management group and commitment of it to the innovation are indispensable to the success of such a project.

He also cited several team and operator problems encountered. They were:

1. The expectations of a small minoriy of employees did not coincide with the demands placed on them by the new plant community. This small group of employees was uncomfortable in group meetings and uneasy in participating in the spontaneous mutual help patterns which prevailed.

2. Some team leaders manifested considerable difficulty in not behaving like traditional authority figures. This difficulty was reinforced by the employees themselves in some instances who seemed actively to seek traditional supervisory responses.

3. The norms covering various aspects of work were evolved by the self-managing work teams themselves, and if an individual failed to conform to these norms, he was subject to excessive peer group pressure.

4. There were some problems that ensued from the shifting of

roles that took place in the plant. Team members were given assignments that were usually limited to supervisors, managers or professionals. This sometimes generated mixed feelings among outsiders who had occasion to deal with persons in the plant. For example, a vendor who customarily made his sales to persons at higher organizational levels registered disappointment when he found he was dealing with a worker.

In Professor Walton's judgment, management had specific expectations concerning anticipated gain from the new plant system: a more reliable, more flexible and lower cost manufacturing plant; a healthier work climate; and learning that could be translated to other corporate units. In his judgment, these goals were met. He cites the following eight factors which facilitated success of the plant:

1. Because of the particular technology and manufacturing processes in this particular business, it was possible by more fully utilizing the human potential of employees to both enhance quality of worklife and reduce costs.

2. It was technically and economically feasible to eliminate some inherently boring work and some of the physically disagreeable tasks.

3. The project had the advantage of being introduced in a new plant staffed by a work force which was hired all at the same time.

4. The physical isolation of the plant from other parts of the company facilitated the development of unique organizational patterns.

5. Because the work force was relatively small, it was possible to achieve individual recognition and identification.

6. The plant was a nonunion plant and thus was unencumbered by constraints that organized labor might have imposed.

7. The technology called for and permitted communication within the work force.

8. Employees were able to form a positive attitude toward the product and the company.

In a March, 1974 update on the Topeka plant, the following tangible results were reported by Edward R. Dulworth, Operations

Manager, in a speech at the UCLA program on "The Changing World of Work."

1. Costs savings range from 20 to 40% greater than other plants in the company. This amounts to savings of about $2 million a year.

2. Regarding quality, rejects are about 80% less than what is normal in the business.

3. There has been no sabotage, theft or worker-caused shutdowns.

4. Absenteeism is about 1%, and 90% of that is with the knowledge and approval of management.

5. Turnover is about 10%. This compares with about 15% for the parent company as a whole. About half of these people (the 10%) have quit and half have been fired.

6. Three times as many employees are taking advantage of outside education opportunities compared with employees in company's other plants.

7. Workers say they like the system, the work, and the opportunities. They are very open about any negatives. They feel they own the plant.

Mr. Dulworth also presented the following summary of problems:

1. The organization of the plant demands openness, honesty and willingness to deal with problems among team members. Many people didn't respond initially to this type of demand, and this is still a problem.

2. The only real performance problem is in getting the workers to keep the plant as clean as it should be.

3. Some persons turned out not to fit well into this type of organization and have left or been fired.

4. There have been some problems to be "worked through" with the parent company, General Foods. Parent company management is uneasy about "who's in control" at Topeka. Also, the organization of the Topeka plant necessitates demands for much data by the teams that heretofore had not been available even to the plant manager—this creates difficulties for the parent company.

5. There has been some trouble getting *managers* to learn to operate in the open type of system that has been established at the Topeka plant. The *workers* love the system.

Comment: Overall evidence shows that permitting employees greater participation in decision making is not restricted to small, special situations in new plants such as Topeka. Other case histories report substantial improvements in both the quality of worklife and productivity in companies both large and small, new and old, unionized and nonunion, and in various parts of the country.

AMERICAN TELEPHONE AND TELEGRAPH

This experimental study was prompted by the fact that, in the 1960s, when the nation's unemployment rate was low, AT&T was experiencing an unusually high turnover in virtually all departments. Jobs were relatively easy to find at the time and there was little to persuade employees to stay on a job they did not find interesting. College recruiters, after listening to the complaints of those leaving the company, told AT&T, "You don't deserve the people we send you."

The turnover rate was particularly high among people who stayed less than six months—employees who left before the company could offset their initial training costs. There was, then, a strong cost motivation to correct this situation.

The initial job enrichment study began in 1965 in AT&T's treasury department. Robert N. Ford, personnel director of work organization and environmental research, in *Motivation Through the Work Itself* (New York, American Management Association, Inc., 1969), listed the objectives of the treasury department experiment as:

1. Improve the quality of service.
2. Maintain or perhaps improve productivity levels.
3. Improve the turnover situation.
4. Lower costs.
5. Improve employee satisfaction in job assignments.

(The project director assumed that if the last objective was accomplished, the preceding four would follow—an assumption not always validated in other studies.)

The initial study group involved 104 women who answered customer complaint letters, plus sixteen women who handled telephoned complaints. The employees were divided into five small groups:

1. Twenty experimentals in what was called the "achieving group" whose assignments would be vertically loaded.
2. The sixteen phone answerers (their uncommitted supervisor decided to make changes similar to those in the experimental group).
3. Twenty women in a control group. The second-level supervisor was asked to ignore the study while the first-level supervisor and the employees were told nothing.
4. Nineteen women in an uncommitted group.
5. Twenty women in another uncommitted group.

It is important to note that none of the women—or the first-level supervisors—were informed of the study in which they participated. The project director acknowledged certain starting points:

1. Remove the sources of job dissatisfaction—poor wages, poor, working conditions, inadequate supervision.
2. But don't expect removing these to make up for boring jobs.
3. If the job is boring, load it with true work motivators: achievement as perceived by the employee, recognition associated with an achievement, more responsibiliy, advancement to a higher order of task, and growth of employee competence.

The project director had warned management there might be an initial drop in productivity and in employee attitudes, and he requested that in spite of this possibility they permit the experiment to run for the full six-month period. Although there was considerable managerial anxiety about the experiment, this support was granted.

In designing the project, the director was eager to differentiate between horizontal and vertical job loading. Horizontal loading, he explained to top level supervisors, meant simply enlarging a job or rearranging its parts without making it more challenging. The following suggestions for horizontal loading for the department were proposed and rejected:

1. Setting firm quotas of letters to be answered each day.

2. Channeling all difficult complex inquiries to a few women so that the remainder might attain high rates of output.

3. Rotating the women through the telephone units to units handling different customers and then back to their own units.

4. Letting the girls type the letters themselves, as well as compose them, or take on other clerical functions, such as reviewing the files or obtaining detailed information.

"Obviously this type of loading does not really improve the task, but it is unquestionably aimed at this end," observed Ford. "We often turn completely away from a bad job assignment and attempt to make the work tolerable by improving rest rooms, adding soft music, subtracting time worked via coffee breaks and so on. In effect, these moves say: 'This work is boring but it must be done. Please do it and we'll try to reduce the level of pain.'"

Focusing on what could be done to make the job itself more challenging, the following list of changes was agreed upon by the project director and top-level supervisors for the achieving group:

1. Subject matter experts were appointed within each unit for other members of the unit to consult with before seeking supervisory help. (Later on it was found that the girls had rearranged these assignments among themselves along lines they felt to be more meaningful. This was a real test of the climate of responsibility the company was trying to build and it was accepted as such by the management.)

2. Correspondents were told to sign their own names to letters from the very first day on the job after training. Previously the verifier or supervisor usually signed for many months.

3. The work of the more experienced correspondents was looked over less frequently by supervisors, and this was done at each correspondent's desk. Instead of verifying 100% of the let-

ters, the proportion was reduced to 10%, a source of significant dollar savings.

4. Less rather than more pressure was placed upon the group for production.

5. Outgoing work went directly to the mailroom without crossing the supervisor's desk.

6. All correspondents were told that they would be held fully accountable for the quality of work—a responsibility previously shared with verifiers and supervisors.

7. Correspondents were encouraged to answer letters in a more personalized way rather than adhering to a standard form letter.

Among the results reported for the first six-month trial period were:

1. All groups within the experiment showed improvement in the quality of customer service, as measured by an index already used in the company, but the experimental groups were well ahead of the others.

2. Turnover was greatly reduced for the two achieving groups, but continued at the former high level for the control group and the two uncommitted groups.

2. Turnover was greatly reduced for the two achieving groups, but continued at the former high level for the control group and the two uncommitted groups.

3. There was a reduction in absences of long duration among the experimental workers: from 2.0% to 1.4%. The control group showed a slight increase in this category of absences.

4. No great emphasis was placed on productivity in measuring results, since it was conceded that it could take from twenty minutes to two days to compose an appropriate letter. However, the experimental groups exceeded previous levels of productivity.

5. Promotions were being made in large proportions out of groups one and two because of their better performance.

6. There was a substantial improvement in job attitude among the achieving group, a lesser improvement in the telephone group, and a deterioration of attitude in the control group and

one of the uncommitted groups. The other uncommitted group showed a slight improvement.

At the time of the final survey, members of the achieving group reported they now derived greater satisfaction from the job and felt their performance had improved because of this. Achieving supervisors found fewer crises, few necessities for repeat calls, and higher group morale demonstrated by group enthusiasm toward work problems. Achieving group supervisors find that more of their time is now available for actual supervisory work rather than having all their time absorbed by verifying outgoing letters, a responsibility which the girls now accept themselves.

At the end of the six-month trial, top management in AT&T's treasury department set up a small manpower utilization group involving more than 1,150 employees, including several hundred supervisors. A year and a half later, the company estimated that the program had saved $558,000.

On the basis of its successes in the treasury department, AT&T then conducted eighteen additional studies at various companies within the Bell System. A variety of departments were included: engineering, traffic, plant, controllers, and commercial (service representatives). While it is impossible to describe all these programs in detail, it can be stated that good results were reported throughout the system. None of the projects had the impressive results found at the treasury department, but there were substantial improvements in the commercial departments, and visible, consistently good results with the controllers.

Early in 1968, the top management of the Bell System decided to take employee motivation programs out of the special trial projects class and include them as part of their ongoing program of development. As Ford notes: "This is, in a very real sense, the most substantial proof of the success of the projects to date."

In his book on the AT&T experiments, Ford points out the need to distinguish between corporate purpose and individual employee purpose, and to concentrate upon helping the employee meet his job needs. The worker is deeply committed to serving the customer only when he is simultaneously meeting his own needs. When these needs are met, the employee will serve management well because he has his own little part ot the business to run, not because of attempts to motivate him from outside his own frame of needs.

Ford concluded: "The data from these studies show that it is possible to get an order-of-magnitude change, not just a small increment. Modern employees are bright, healthy, well-fed and well-educated compared to those in the time-and-motion study days. They will not accept dull jobs unless the jobs are their very own. We must set the conditions of work so as to gradually maximize the responsibility thrust upon the worker. To do this we must ask ourselves:

What do I do for him that he could now do for himself?

What thinking can he now do for himself?

What goals could we now set *jointly*?

What advanced training or skill could he now have?

What job could he work toward now? How could I help him?

Is there a way of combining this job with another one he would like? Is the module right?

Is there anything he does that could be given to a lower-rated job?

"We must learn to trade off engineering economies for human values and not to assume that this will be costly. . . .We will know that we are doing something right if we can change the conditions of the job so that employees will stay on and work productively. . . . The way to achieve this end, for new or old employees, is not to confront them with demands, but to confront them with demanding, meaningful work. And the employees will always have the last word as to whether the work is meaningful."

Comment: AT&T is one of the largest companies, if not the largest, in the United States. Job enrichment efforts have the support of the president and are spreading slowly through the company. How well this works will depend largely on the receptiveness of local managers and department heads.

In the Bell System the guiding philosophy has been to give the employee every part of the job that he or she is able to handle in the area bearing upon the employee-customer relationship. At the moment the company believes job enrichment should be confined to this area.

PROCTER AND GAMBLE

Several Procter and Gamble plants have been experimenting with an overall job design and enrichment system involving teams. In each shift, one complete team, made up of different work groups, is made responsible for a given type of production. For example:

LIQUIDS

Making   Packing   Shipping

Up and down the line, there is full and free communication of production information. The team meetings not only permit but value expressions of feelings and perceptions as well as task-oriented problem solving. Problems are discussed until there is consensus acceptance of the decision. Each work group has a measurable desired outcome which is stated in terms of cost, quantity, quality and level of appearance.

Writing on "Democracy in the Factory," in *The Atlantic*, April 1973, David Jenkins says: "Without doubt the most radical organizational changes made on a practical day-to-day basis in the United States have taken place at Procter & Gamble...well known for its hard-boiled, aggressive management practices."

The focus of Jenkins' report is the Procter & Gamble plant in Lima, Ohio. Interviewed by Jenkins, Charles Krone, the head of organizational development at Procter & Gamble's Cincinnati headquarters, said: "The plant was designed from the ground up to be democratic. The technology—the location of instruments, for example— was designed to stimulate relationships between people, to bring about autonomous group behavior, and to allow people to affect their own environment."

Jenkins continued: "The basic principle is that the human being **has growth potential. And a key to the design and operation of the plant is that no barriers should be placed to hinder that growth.**

"Just as there are no physical barriers, so there are no barriers between jobs. Indeed, there are no jobs at all in the ordinary sense.... Not everybody can do every job, but every member of the community is constantly adding to his own skills in some specialized field. 'You might be a laboratory technician,' Krone says, 'but you also handle operating jobs. Everybody carries the same minimum responsibility. No matter where you go, you always have to go back to the operation— you cannot become exclusively the specialist.'

"The workers have virtually complete control of the plant. There are no time clocks or other symbols of petty 'class' distinctions, and everybody is on straight salary. 'The manager,' says Krone, 'has very little decision-making power. Usually, instead of being seen as a resource, he is seen as an invader, fulfilling a directive and controlling role—there is much less of that here.' . . . I asked Krone if he and his fellow managers gave the employees complete financial figures. 'Well, no,' he answered, 'they give them to us. One guy is interested in accounting and develops all that information. They draw up their own budgets, and so on.'

"The plant's hard data are in fact easily understandable. Even though the pay scale is considerably higher than is customary, overall costs are approximately half those of a conventional plant. Much of this is because of the advanced technology. But this technology could not function properly if there were not, at the same time, an advanced social system. Quality is also affected, Krone told me: 'It has the most outstanding quality record of any plant we have—it is virtually perfect quality.'

"The results have, in fact, been so good that the open systems principles have been applied in a number of other new Procter & Gamble plants constructed over the past few years, and the employees in such plants now total almost 10% of the company's 28,000 U.S. employees. . . . The open-systems methods have proved quite profitable, so it is likely that this figure will rise in the future."

CRYOVAC DIVISION, W. R. GRACE & CO.

This report, entitled "Organizational Redesign: A Study in Transition," was prepared for McGraw-Hill, Inc. in April 1973 by Robert M. Frame, Manager of Personnel and Organization Development, Camarillo Operations, Cryovac Division, W. R. Grace & Co.

In 1968, the Cryovac Division of W. R. Grace & Company made a decision to open its first West Coast manufacturing facility, and following plant site surveys in several locations, Camarillo, California was selected. Viewing itself as an innovator in employee relations, this leader in heat-shrink plastic packaging material production conducted a study designed to get at the motivational potential of opening this sixth plant in the 2,000-employee Cryovac organization along lines paralleling behavioral-science-based concepts. Initial interest centered in the fostering of a participative approach to management which would hopefully avoid sources of employee dissatisfaction identified by behaviorists. Of special interest was a growing trend to place blue-collar workers on salaried status, consistent with efforts to foster feelings of mutual trust and respect.

Cryovac interviewed a number of all-salaried firms as it developed the following philosophy to govern management at the new Camarillo plant:

> A belief that the potential for innovative or creative contribution is widely distributed in the working population.
>
> A belief that most people want to do a good job and will if they are given the opportunity.
>
> A belief that most people flourish and improve in value to the organization when given increased responsibility commensurate with their capabilities.
>
> A belief that a maximally effective organization is achievable only through the development of a comprehensive program of human resource management.

Translated into operational terms, these beliefs included: conversion to a unified system of compensation for all nonexempt employees; elimination of time clocks and job titles which might be perceived as demeaning; reduction of differences in both policy and philosophy treating exempt vs nonexempt personnel; development of personnel policies consistent with assumptions about human nature... primarily those of mutual respect and trust in key areas; and finally, acceptance of the need to develop and implement—"at the earliest practicable date consistent with plant start-up"—a systematic program of job enrichment.

Looking back, at that time, the phrase "job enrichment" was

merely a buzz-word to the newly-formed management team put together from several points on the company compass. The many pressures and problems of plant start-up notwithstanding, the group did hold several weeks of regular discussion regarding the philosophy of management they intended to implement and the hoped-for benefits.

Top management backed off and took a good look. It then began to dimly realize that the real potential in human resource maximization lay not in dealing with the environment or *context* within which the basic jobs were performed. Rather it lay in the *content* of those jobs. And while most of the operational plans outlined above had been worked at with some vigor, the key element—the redesign, rearrangement, or restructure of tasks so that they were more interesting and challenging and provided more opportunities for growth, achievement, greater responsibility and self-control—was missing. With only moderate differences, the Camarillo jobs were identical to those in the older company plants. Superimposing salaried status for direct labor personnel into this environment was not likely to produce desired motivational and productivity results at all. Nor was, however sincere, lip service to management philosophy, apparently interpreted by supervision as permissiveness, the answer. Professional help was indicated.

Because of the highly specialized technologies in the plant—extruded saran tubing, flexographic tubing, and special-design bag making—it was decided that an analytical approach to job enrichment which incorporated both engineering and behavioral science was critical. An associate and former student of Frederick Herzberg who had been consulted early in the planning was brought back into the picture. He, in turn, called upon an international expert in the Socio-Technical Systems approach, located within a reasonable distance of the Camarillo plant.

The former reiterated that "Job Enrichment" is essentially a strategy for utilizing more fully the talents and competencies of employees by placing in their hands as much decision making and responsibility as they can handle. The latter—agreeing with the above—added another dimension to the process of analysis of the plant's problem: He pointed out that in a technologically sophisticated environment like that at Camarillo, before turning over decision making and self-control to employees with the aforementioned hoped-for results, management had to be certain what the sources of variance in quality and productivity really were.

The Job Design Team Is Formed

To launch the program the end-line process department ("Bag-making") was selected. It had the most labor-intensive process and contributed the greatest process cost to the product. Not only was probability of success good due to greater human resources, but program impact would be highly visible.

A job enrichment team was selected composed of the first-line supervisors in the department in question. With the initial help of the outside consultants, the team members first studied job rede-sign philosophy and then met for a full day weekly for some twenty weeks. Utilizing the Herzberg approach initially, they brainstormed ideas for making the work more meaningful, gener-ating over a hundred possibilities in the first session alone. These were set aside for a time and the sociotechnical analysis-of-vari-ance approach described above was employed to pinpoint the many sources of technical problems impacting upon the basic tasks and hence upon employees. Beginning at the end of the pro-duction process and working backwards from symptom to cause the team initially defined some 150 key variables which in turn were screened down to 48 "super" variables. These were in turn analyzed and the criteria by which the hypotheses were screened for final inclusion in the new job structure were as follows:

Is it motivating? That is...

> Does it offer increased challenge to the incumbent?
> Does it provide a more complete task?
> Does it contribute to a logical work "module," with a visible beginning and end?
> Does it offer real-time feedback opportunity on how well the job is being done?
> Does it give the incumbent greater control over the work, including decision making?

New Job Structures Are Developed

Once the "variance analysis" hypotheses surviving the above

screen were combined with those resulting from general enrich-ment brainstorming, a new job structure was developed. Work "modules" were ranked from low-to-high degree of difficulty and responsibility, consistent with natural training approaches required for the new employee entering the new job "ladder" on the bottom rung.

The issue of promotion and compensation arose early. The final policies developed incorporated a principle of promotion and pay based on demonstrated skills proficiency. With few constraints, an employee could progress as fast and as far up the training lad-der as individual ability and motivation would allow. Training and compensation were thus individualized. Qualification at higher levels of proficiency was in turn directly related to compensation. Performance Reviews were developed to incorporate both con-siderable objective data available on individual productivity and the principle of evaluation-by mutually-established objectives be-tween employee and supervisor.

Shift Manning Changes

Once final job structures were developed the Job Enrichment Team developed an action plan for making the transaction to a new shift manning mode. The experimental end-process Bag-making Department made the transition from a three-on-two manning mode, with one male operator and two female inspector-packers manning two machines, to a one-on-one mode where all but two employees were encouraged to learn the *entire* machine operation and handle it alone. This was done via a six-level hier-archy of skill through which an operator was given opportunity to progress as fast as his or her ability to take advantage of training would allow. Compensation was thereby tied directly to contribu-tion since pay adjustments were made immediately upon demon-stration of proficiency at the next higher "rung" on the job ladder.

The Program is Expanded

In early 1972, several key events occurred, resulting in the Cama-rillo program being extended to all major departments plantwide. Camarillo's job enrichment program was to become not merely an experiment in reducing worker alienation to boring tasks, with hoped-for benefits in employee satisfaction and productivity. Rather, it was to enlarge to a comprehensive, systematic approach to cost-effective management plantwide. Plant management had come to realize that significant progress in the redesign of jobs could only occur in a climate of organizational change wherein no department lines were sacred.

For example: A job design team struggling with machine maintenance problems would be severely restricted in creating the optimum organization of tasks and assignments if they felt that the critical change lay not merely in restructuring production tasks, but in changing the reporting of the maintenance technicians to one where they worked both for and with the production supervisor, rather than reporting to an outside staff department. Following the transition, the maintenance force became an integral part of the production team, reporting directly to the production shift supervisor.

Plant management learned that jurisdictional conflict between production departments served only to reduce efficiency and constrain organizational development. Solution: Encourage job redesign teams elsewhere in the plant not to concern themselves with these artificial barriers to optimum human resource utilization. How?...by simply eliminating the barriers themselves. As management promotions to other operations occurred, opportunity to merge the remaining two production departments (Printing and Extrusion) presented itself.

Next, plantwide coordination of the newly developing approach to management was established. Each line and staff department was encouraged to begin discussion of its particular opportunities, needs, and problems in manpower utilization...and to follow what had by now become a systematic step-by-step program for human resource management which went far beyond mere delegation of greater decision-making control to employees.

Capitalizing on the experience and mistakes of the experimental group, a new job design team in the newly-formed Press/Extrusion Department began work in the spring of 1972. Preliminary analysis of results of the initial March 1971 organization and machine-manning mode vs that of August 1972 show first- and second-level supervision was reduced by 50% with the new department under the direction of only one production superintendent. As with Bagmaking, the maintenance work force reporting direction was changed to one directly under line management. The resultant before-and-after total reduction in work force is thus reflected: from 15.5 nonexempt and 6 exempt personnel involved per shift, to 12.5 nonexempt and 2 exempt.

Such a dramatic change was not without its problems, particularly during a period when production volume pressures were increasing sharply. (In March 1971, the average units per day volume was 250,000. By August 1972, it had increased to 420,000. By April 1973, it was close to 500,000.)

To offset understandable feelings of threat associated with such change, the new job design team elected to involve the employees in plans for said change to a much greater degree. A series of meetings were held to invite reaction to and suggestions for anticipated changes in both organization and job content. By this time, many rumors were flying about the initial program in Bagmaking and the meetings minimized these, while at the same time improving acceptance of change on the part of operating personnel.

The absence of any major morale or production problem in Bagmaking, coupled with the aggressive support reflected by both the Plant Manager and his successor, greatly assisted the team of supervisors to internalize the principles involved while reducing feelings of insecurity about their own future roles. This was perceived by most of them as *their* program—one designed essentially to free them from production "firefighting" to become full-fledged shift managers by pushing down decision-making authority over production problems to the lowest level in the organization. While this did not erase feelings of ambivalence about the many challenges discovered in giving employees greater freedom and authority of action than ever before, it tended to minimize feelings of insecurity on the part of supervision about their own futures . . . a problem common to almost all reported experiments along these lines.

Results to Date

There have been overall organizational changes in the management structure as a result of the program. A Quality Control Manager position was eliminated because early in the program it became clear that one opportunity available was to eliminate inspectors who, after all, could not inspect quality into the product. Placing in the hands of the operator controls and data-giving real-time feedback on his quality proved the solution to many quality problems. This enabled the plant to eliminate by attrition a number of Q.C. inspectors and to merge the Q.C. function into both line management and operating responsibilities.

A customer account assignment program in Bagmaking was launched to give operators greater identification with the customer using their output. This included visits to customer operations by some operating employees. Integration of the Q.C. function with the operating duties did not result in a deterioration of quality. One key index: flexographic print quality did not deteriorate, with the Camarillo facility winning five out of six print quality awards given on an interplant competitive basis bimonthly beginning in the early fall of 1971.

Other changes include the shift of production control to the direct cognizance of line management, plus the reduction in second level production supervision and the shift in production maintenance from engineering to production mentioned earlier.

Notwithstanding two general wage increases during that period, a 28.6% improvement in units of output per direct labor dollar was achieved between March 1971 and February 1973. During a period when production output rose 68%, overall plant personnel was reduced 9.7%.

The team working currently in the newly-formed Press/Extrusion Department recently outlined the reasons to which they attribute such performance in their area as follows:

> More effective utilization of capital equipment (50% increase in run time capacity).
>
> Increased output (a conservative potential of 50%).
>
> Reduced conflict between operating employees through more direct control over process variance.
>
> Increased skill utilization and flexibility.

Attitude Surveyed

Employee attitudes, as measured in part by a recent anonymous attitude survey, range from sceptical optimism on the part of some who are as yet uncertain of the impact the whole program will make on them in areas where it is only in its infancy, to strong endorsement to the sensitive area of compensation. On this issue the survey reflected that by far the most satisfied group was the Bag-making Department, where the longest experience with the pay-for-skills proficiency concept exists. This same group ranked highest on the survey factor, "opportunity for advancement," and the general feeling of identification with the company, than any other production or maintenance group.

Management attitude is perhaps best reflected in the comments of the new chief executive at the plant: "Effective human resource management is more than a pill labeled 'job enrichment'," says plant manager R. B. Fenyves. "Only when you begin to sense that it's the only sensible way to run a business and not merely another personnel program to make employees 'happy' does this style of management cease to be merely a 'buzz word'. We're not ready to export our program yet...in fact, we may never suggest other company units duplicate it at all because it must be customized to fit each situation, and they all differ. However, there are definite principles involved which demand hard work on the part of everyone. The program must cut across traditional thinking about total organization before the real potential can be tapped. Hence, it is a slow process but one with a measurable payout in benefits for everyone concerned."

Conclusion

Based on the experience at that point, local Cryovac management believed that several conclusions could be drawn:

1. Salaried status for blue-collar workers is not in and of itself a motivational program, despite its contribution to minimizing dissatisfaction with differential treatment.
2. If introduced into an otherwise unchanged organizational climate such an investment is unlikely to produce hoped-for results in reduced employee alienation or measurable performance improvement.

3. Job enrichment, participative decision making, and other similar programs aimed at dealing with a young work force demanding more meaning from employment plus the ever-present pressure for cost-effective human resource utilization are relatively inadequate *by themselves* to achieve the very ambitious program objectives outlined earlier.

4. The most powerful solution is to integrate such programs into an overall systematic and ongoing organization design effort, one which takes advantage of every personnel change and views it against the background of a master human resource blueprint.

5. The above implies at best enthusiastic top management support or at worst a "hands off" agreement until and unless any experimental group appears clearly in serious trouble. Only in an organizational climate essentially free of serious doubts about top management interference or support can the grass roots work progress effectively.

GENERAL ELECTRIC

This report has been prepared from material provided by General Electric Company.

General Electric reported on a series of studies of employee motivation carried out by its Behavioral Research Service. An exploratory study reported on in 1966, in "Achieving Productive Motivation Through Job Design," stated:

Many jobs in the factory are designed in such a way that it is almost impossible for the individual to evaluate the real worth of his contribution....Surveys have shown that hourly workers in many jobs feel that their work has little or no meaning and just seems to go on and on endlessly in a monotonous manner. This kind of work not only generates feelings of boredom, apathy, fatigue and dissatisfaction, but also leads to resentment and active resistance. Workmanship suffers, employee turnover becomes a serious problem, and work stoppages, slow-downs and strikes disrupt production.

In this study, the researchers attempted to measure the effects of various design characteristics on employee attitudes about their jobs, and quality of workmanship. Manufacturing shop operations and quality control managers in five departments were asked to identify work groups that were consistently high or consistently low in quality of output. Then, 25 groups at the high end of the quality continuum and 25 groups at the low end were selected for study.

The foreman of each of the designated groups was interviewed for information on job-related factors such as cycle time, size of work group, training, repetitiveness. In addition, a few employees from each work group, randomly selected by the researcher, were asked to complete a brief questionnaire dealing with pride in work, job meaningfulness, sense of accomplishment, monotony, identification with the product and the company, and attitudes toward management.

Because of the exploratory nature of the study, the researchers decided they would not attempt to articulate formal findings. Instead, they presented a series of provisional recommendations to the managers of shop operations.

1. Establish a formal training program for hourly employees beyond the required minimum.

2. Create subgoals to measure accomplishment in groups where repetition is high or where the employees do not ordinarily see the finished product.

3. Provide employees with feedback on the quality of their performance on a regular and frequent basis.

4. Have each foreman put continuing effort into the maintenance of a very neat and orderly work area.

5. Arrange work areas to either make co-workers' conversation very easy while working, or make it virtually impossible for employees to converse while working.

6. Increase the number of operations performed by an employee whenever possible.

7. Structure jobs so that workers can, at least occasionally, move about the work area.

8. Explore ways to assign greater personal responsibilities to an individual.

Some of the recommendations of the foregoing study were further explored in a 1967 report entitled "Motivating the Hourly Employee." In assessing productive motivation, the company took into account the following attitudinal dimensions:

Attitudes or feelings about the work itself (job content):

Enjoys work versus bored with work
Pride in workmanship
Sense of accomplishment

Attitudes or feelings about the work environment (job context):

Perceived relationship between personal needs and department or company goals
Identification with the department or company products
Perception of general management
Perception of immediate supervisor

These attitudes, in the opinion of the researchers, exert a direct influence on:

1. Productivity—quantity to meet customer demand
2. Quality of work—workmanship to keep customer satisfied
3. Labor relations—a working environment which minimizes income loss to employee and company

The study undertook to observe and measure the following variables:

Responsibility for own work (the extent to which an individual can use his own discretion)

Shift work—repetitiveness of the work (a function of cycle time and the number of operations)

Physical activity (is it sedentary work or does an employee move about area, use physical energy, etc?)

Rotation between work stations—goals (in terms of eventual use of product, customer, logical number of units to produce, etc.)

Group structure (small work groups at interdependent stations versus individual work stations relatively independent of each other)

Role training (any informal or formal program which promotes insights into the importance of the job and encourages psychological investment in the work)

The following results were reported:

1. Productive motivation was higher where employees had some discretionary responsibility in their jobs.
2. Second shift employees had more favorable attitudes than first shift employees.
3. Productive motivation was lower for employees in highly repetitive jobs.
4. Regularly scheduled rotation is reacted to favorably while casual rotation has the opposite effect.
5. The opportunity for relatively vigorous physical activity on the job is associated with greater productive motivation.
6. Opportunities for social interaction seldom resulted in more favorable attitudes toward the job.
7. Role-training and participation resulted in significant improvement in overall productive motivation.

In a third study, "The Effect of Employee Involvement on Work Performance," which was carried out by Personnel Research and reported on in 1969, General Electric explored the concept of stewardship. According to the report, "Stewardship denotes something more than merely adding responsibility. It implies having pride in doing the work properly, maintaining a sustained alertness for job improvements in all aspects of job-related functions, and a willingness to accept responsibility for related tasks which one has not previously or typically covered."

In one program, employees participated in a role-training program to help them understand how their work affected other groups in the plant. They were given a better understanding of the entire manufacturing process, the importance of each step in the process, and the problems encountered in producing the product. Each work group was taken on a tour of local businesses where their products were used.

Each operator was informed of the total output required for his unit, then asked to use this information to determine the order in which he would work on each of several items. Stewardship was developed further by prominently posting each day in the work area a graph depicting group performance to schedule. This provided performance results feedback. On the basis of this information, operators were encouraged to set their own quality goals in the form of defect per operator.

As a result of this program there were significant performance improvements. Defects per operator were reduced approximately 50% and productivity, based on dollar output results, rose from a 25.7 average for the nine months before the program, to a 46.7 average after its introduction.

In another aspect of the same program, the sequential assembly process was modified so that a single operator continued down the entire line with one production unit. This changeover in assembly substantially reduced the number of defects per completed units. There was also an improvement in productivity, from 40 units, the monthly average produced in the nine months before the changeover, to 52 units in the first month after the change, 60 in the second and 71 in the third.

Another example of the effects of added responsibility and a feeling of stewardship toward the job came in a department where most hourly employees were semiskilled equipment operators. In-line inspectors were taken off the floor and operators were asked to do their own inspection. In assuming the self-inspection responsibility, the operators became more alert to quality and scheduling problems. As a result, quality improved and the cost of direct labor was reduced. The self-inspection resulted in approximately a 25% reduction in the cost of product failures during the first year. The improved performance was sustained throughout the following two years.

In presenting its conclusions, the GE report stated:

> Several conditions must be met if efforts to improve the motivation of workers are to be successful. In the first place, the program must be conducted by the immediate supervisors of the employees. An outside researcher, or

even a local staff man, cannot conduct such a program successfully.

Secondly, the program cannot be based on a few mechanically applied gimmicks which would hopefully improve performance in some magical way. To be successful, such a program must be based on a genuine desire on the part of the supervisor to build the self-esteem of employees by demonstrating genuine trust and faith in their motives and in their abilities to contribute constructively to the objectives of the work group.

A third important condition of the success of a motivational program is that it must be carried out in an atmosphere of approval. It must not be seen by employees as any kind of admonishment for performance in the past. A punitive attitude on the part of the supervisor will only threaten, rather than build, the self-esteem of the employees. A natural reaction to a threat to one's self-esteem is to become defensive—to defend one's past performance and thus become unconstructive about possible improvement.

General Electric Worker Teams

As reported in *Business Week* of September 9, 1972, pp. 143 and 146, General Electric is exploring worker teams. The idea is to identify a task and then assign a group of 5 to 15 people to handle it. The key is to give the group as much responsibility as possible. Meyer cites a group of welders in a fabricating plant where the team approach was tried. The welders were given responsibility for scheduling and planning their work load. They determined, for example, how much time it would take to meet specifications on any items requiring special welding techniques, a job formerly done by methods-and-standards engineers.

The 12 welders were experienced enough to decide which one of them would do a specific job and the time it would take, Meyer says. "The responsibility meant the men had a bigger say in how they did their jobs, and we found that they all became more committed to the work as team members," says Meyer. Methods engineers are now freed to work on new product models while the welders decide how the daily work is going to be done. The efficiency and quality of work, Meyer adds, has improved significantly, because the team has a real stake in the outcome.

Another approach at GE involves encouraging supervisors and foremen to use "an alternate way" in dealing with workers. The program involves role-playing, and the foreman plays the role of a worker. He may act out a situation where a worker is called in by his superior to discuss a problem, anything from poor work habits to absenteeism. The scene is video-taped and the other supervisors in the training session become critics for the action.

Some 2,000 GE foremen and supervisors have participated in the training sessions, which run three to four hours. According to Meyer, most men who have gone through the sessions go away with the feeling that they can be more effective in their jobs if they put aside a "tough guy" image. "We're not trying to change a foreman's behavior with a lot of theory," says Meyer. "We're saying that there is more to his job than just clobbering people when they get out of line, which is the way a shop has traditionally been run."

As elementary as the lesson may appear, the results have been surprising. In one GE electronic components plant, a group of foremen went through the training. Ten weeks later, the workers they were supervising were performing at a level 20% higher in productive efficiency. Now all the foremen in the plant are taking the training.

TRW SYSTEMS

> This report was published in *Business Week* of September 9, 1972; pp. 143 and 146.

The techniques for changing the attitudes of both management and workers vary from company to company. Since the early 1960s, TRW has used a heavy dose of job enrichment and organization development with both salaried and hourly workers to "produce a climate in which people can share their ideas and get them rammed up through the system," says Dr. Thomas A. Wickes, TRW's director of organizational development.

TRW's experience with project teams has been equally encouraging. "Since we started paying attention to it, projects seem to get started faster, and we seem to come up with more elegant solutions than we did in past, whether it is a manufacturing or a management problem," says Wickes. "We're convinced that in terms of productivity, the man who is most productive is the one who has a real piece of the action. He's in a job where he has control and influence, and one where he is measured on results."

TRW created in one of its manufacturing plants a group it terms a "semiautonomous work team." The workers were given the responsibility of assembling a product as a team rather than separately performing assembly-line tasks. Once they were given the new assignment, they were allowed to schedule their own time as long as they did the job.

One result was the elimination of different shifts for a given job, since it made no sense to work as a team unless its members worked at the same time. Working hours were staggered when necessary to fit personal requirements, and management started to see team members take on tasks formerly regarded as the "company's responsibility." Older, more experienced workers were voluntarily spending time in training younger team members, for example. While the novelty of the new setup may account for the enthusiasm of the group, it is a hard fact that productivity has gone up 15%.

Within TRW, the Systems Group is concerned with advanced products and services, and its organizational approach is correspondingly sophisticated. The following description of it is provided by Sheldon Davis, Vice President of Industrial Relations, TRW Systems.

Systems Group conceives its organization as a total system of interfacing jobs, projects, spans of control, responsibilities, and relationships of people. There exist a large number of complex critical interdependencies. No one technical or administrative group is complete in itself. In getting a particular job done—for example a project, the various resources throughout the company have to be called on to contribute. This requires an organization that affords a continuous open access between individuals and groups.

To help achieve these objectives TRW Systems has incorporated many behavior science concepts in its operating style. The aim of this effort is the creation of an environment that encourages individual flexibility and increased interpersonal competence which is seen as a requisite to the need for constant change and innovation. The behavioral science application is centered around problem solving and task accomplishment. Methods and techniques used at TRW Systems are not viewed as a single experimental program but as an ongoing process that is designed to reach the willingness and needs of individuals and the organization alike.

Today there are numerous identifiable applications of behavioral science in the organization. The following stand out most prominently:

Matrix Organization: A project management system in which a work team is put together based upon required expertise. A person may belong to several teams at once or he may start on a project and then move to another because of his special expertise or because the project manager has asked for the individual or because the employee himself finds the work of the second team more attractive, or the employee may have completed that phase of the program for which his expertise was required. This provides some option for the employee to match the opportunity to his needs at the time which includes an assessment in terms of his total self, his life-style, his goals and objectives.

Internal and External Behavioral Science Consulting Teams: A permanent group of consulting behavioral scientists work with various levels of management, segments of the organization and employee work groups both off-site and on-site.

Team Building: Team building involves a process wherein a manager meets with his work group for extended periods of time to identify and resolve problems directly related to their working as a team.

Intergroup Team Building: A step beyond team building in which interfacing and interdependent work groups (including customer work groups) meet to identify and resolve mutual problems.

Ongoing Diagnosis: Organizing process to evaluate the health of the organization and its climate, and to facilitate communication. In addition to traditional questionnaire techniques, a process called "sensing" is employed. Appropriate individuals are brought together face-to-face so that an individual or group may get a reading on a particular problem area, or segment of the organization. For example, the president periodically meets with and listens while persons directly involved in carrying out projects or programs discuss problems and progress.

Individual Effectiveness: Numerous techniques for developing greater competence in interpersonal skills, including T-Group training, awareness training, etc., particularly as they relate to leadership and managerial effectiveness. Additionally career development workshops are designed to increase individual motivation toward achieving career goals.

There are of course numerous other activities which reflect the direct applications of behavioral science concepts within the organization. Those mentioned here, however, seem most directly related to the subject of organizational productivity and effectiveness.

No formal effort has been established to quantitatively measure the direct impact of any of these techniques in terms of productivity. However, over the years a culture has evolved in which managers at all levels of the organization continue to use the techniques described. Project managers continually call upon the use of Organization Development techniques and resources to work with project teams which seem to get started faster, seem to produce more elegant solutions and come to quicker and more effective conclusions. The influences of these efforts are apparent, for example, in the manner salaries are administered, budgets are developed, planning occurs, etc. TRW Systems management is convinced that individual productivity, creativity, etc. are significantly greater in an atmosphere in which people can share their ideas and have the sense of contribution and participation.

Bibliography

Argyris, C., *Personality and Organizations.* New York: Harper 1957.

Argyris, C., *Integrating the Individual and the Organization.* New York: John Wiley & Sons, 1964.

Blake, R. R., and Mouton, J. S., *Group Dynamics: Key to Decision Making.* Houston: Gulf Publishing Co., 1961.

Campbell, J., Dunnette, M. D., Lawler, E., & Weick, K. E. *Managerial Behavior, Performance and Effectiveness.* New York: McGraw-Hill, 1970.

Davis, L. E., and Taylor, eds. *The Design of Jobs.* London: Penguin Books, 1972.

Ford, R. N., *Motivation Through the Work Itself.* New York: American Management Association, 1969.

Frank, L. L., and Hackman, J. R., *A Failure of Job Enrichment: The Case of the Change That Wasn't.* Technical Report No. 8. Department of Administrative Sciences, Yale University, 1975.

Hackman, J. R., Oldham, G. R., Janson, R., and Purdy, K., *A New Strategy for Job Enrichment.* Technical Report No. 3. Department of Administrative Sciences, Yale University, 1974.

Herzberg, F., *Work and the Nature of Man.* Cleveland: World Publishing, 1966.

Herzberg, F., Mausner, B., and Snyderman, B., *The Motivation to Work.* New York: Wiley, 1959.

Jenkins, G. D., *Job Power.* New York: Doubleday & Co., 1973. (Also Penguin Books, 1974).

Katzell, R. A., and Yankelovich, D., et al., *Work, Productivity and Job Satisfaction.* New York: Psychological Corp., 1975.

Lawler, E., *Pay and Organizational Effectiveness: A Psychological View.* New York: McGraw-Hill, 1971.

Likert, R., *New Patterns of Management*. New York: McGraw-Hill, 1961.

Likert, R., *The Human Organization*. New York: McGraw-Hill, 1967.

Maher, J. R., ed., *New Perspectives in Job Enrichment*. New York: Van Nostrand-Reinhold, 1971.

Marrow, Alfred J., *The Failure of Success*. New York: AMACOM, 1972.

Maslow, A. H., *Motivation and Personality*. New York: Harper, 1970.

McGregor, D., *The Human Side of Enterprise*. New York: McGraw-Hill, 1960.

Richards, M. D., and Greenlow, P. S., *Management: Decisions and Behavior*. Homewood, IL: Irwin, 1972.

Rosow, J. M. (ed.), *The Worker and the Job: Coping with Change*. Englewood Cliffs, NJ: Prentice-Hall, 1974.

Rush, H.M.F., *Behavioral Science: Concepts and Management Applications*. New York: The Conference Board, 1969.

Taylor, F. W., *The Principles of Scientific Management*. New York: Harper, 1911.

U.S. Department of Health, Education and Welfare Task Force, *Work in America*. Cambridge, MA: MIT Press, 1972.

Vroom, Victor H., *Work and Motivation*. New York: John Wiley and Sons, 1964.

Vroom, Victor H., and Yetton, Phillip W., *Leadership and Decision Making*. Pittsburgh: University of Pittsburgh Press, 1973.

Whyte, W. F. (ed.), *Money and Motivation: An Analysis of Incentives in Industry*. New York: Harper, 1955.